Testimonials & Comments

"Companies and Executives are always searching for relevant research that captures the present and future state of the workplace. This report by MBM is not only relevant, it is timely because we are facing a transition in organizations. Employees desire a people-centric company to work for and grow with more than any other facet a company can offer. MBM's research shows we have quite a gap to cross to move from people-centricity being aspirational to a tangible reality. Every page of this report is invaluable and will be a constant resource to refer to often."

Steve Browne
Chief People Officer LaRosa's, Inc

 https://www.linkedin.com/in/steveb5/

"This makes a fascinating and insightful read for anyone seeking clarity on the value awarded to the extraordinary humans toiling in the global corporate economy. This report is an awesome exposé".

Andrew Stotter-Brooks
Chief Learner at Weird Human,
Award-Winning L&D Professional

https://www.linkedin.com/in/andrewstotts/

"To survive and thrive today, every business need a competitive advantage, in their product/service and in their people. In consulting and training with more than 1000 companies worldwide, I have found that, consistently, the quality of their people, and the way they are respected and valued, is the ultimate competitive advantage".

Brian Tracy
President of Brian Tracy International

https://www.linkedin.com/in/briantracyinternational/

Testimonials & Comments

"Having seen this in many of the companies I consult for who talk about their people focus yet don't mention them once in their reporting, I hope leaders will see this MBM report as a wakeup call: to boost profits, we must prioritize people genuinely. Despite talking the talk, many companies need to improve in walking the walk, especially in leadership. True success is not just about saying but doing—bridging the gap between words and actions. In the dance of profit and people, authentic leadership transforms intentions into a thriving reality."

Kim-Adele Randall
CEO - Authentic Achievements

 https://www.linkedin.com/in/kimadele/

"This report by MBM is a fascinating read for all of us who are passionate about the value of human capital. When annual reports focus solely on financial gains without addressing the welfare of the workforce, it sends a clear message that the company's priorities are skewed. This not only risks eroding employee morale but also tarnishes the company's image in the eyes of consumers and stakeholders, which is short-sighted in today's socially conscious environment. I really hope this eye-opening read makes leaders sit up and take notice!".

Kate Cousens
Co-Founder DICE Business

 https://www.linkedin.com/in/katecousens/

"Here we go then........"Does my bum look big in this" and "How important are your people" are two classic questions that elicit dodgy replies. "Our most important asset is our people," this tired old cliche is put firmly into context by this brilliant report, which then shows how really important your people are."

Geoff Burch
Business Author, and the Alternative Business Guru

 https://www.linkedin.com/in/geoff-burch-73754821/

"A fascinating snapshot of businesses walking their talk - starting by defining their talk! Wellbeing, coaching, leadership, learning, DEI, and people ... an essential focus with a huge ripple effect that includes, ultimately, profit!"

Dr Tara Halliday
Specialist Executive Coach for Imposter Syndrome

 https://www.linkedin.com/in/tara-halliday-phd/

Testimonials & Comments

"This sprawling piece of research offers some interesting findings and perspectives that may help to inform your thinking on where your organization should place its priorities."

James M. Kerr

Top-Ranked Leadership and Culture Expert Author of Indispensable: Build and Lead A Company Your Customers Can't Live Without

in https://www.linkedin.com/in/james-kerr-09a70bb/

"Employers who can find the balance between people and profits are always going to be more successful than those who cannot. Long term, positive and happy work environments breeds an environment of familiarity, confidence and innovation. Those environments are created when employers are dedicated to fostering growth among their staff, building their skills and confidence, as well as helping employees determine what career paths they want to take…then ensuring they have opportunities in house. If employees can retain staff, pay them fairly and provide opportunities for growth, we may see a much needed resurgence in loyalty and dedication among employees that's sorely lacking in todays employment landscape. Jobs have been whittled down to nothing more than a business transaction where there's no buy in, no emotional connection and no loyalty between employees and employers. Yes, profits are important, but when you put people first, you'll always be successful."

Robynn Storey

CEO of Storeyline Resumes, Pioneer of Innovative Executive Resume Writing and Holistic Career Services

in https://www.linkedin.com/in/robynnstorey/

"This report provides a fantastic resource for those genuinely interested in creating a people over profit culture - and demonstrates the huge gap between what we say and what we practice. The words we use in our organisation and in our organisational collateral must be in alignment with our people strategies and goals, without this alignment, organisations are in danger of being viewed as taking a performative approach to their people agenda. What is particularly striking, is the comparison of wellbeing words and EDI words used (or not!) in the Top 100 companies annual reports, with an average of 4 wellbeing words used. This report brings this to life with a fascinating reveal of the Top 100 Companies use of profit words over people words: a must read for all People People!"

Michelle Hartley
Founder People Sorted

 https://www.linkedin.com/in/michellehartleyfinderofawesome/

Testimonials & Comments

"This report brings to life the increasingly prevalent conversations I am having with business leaders the world over. Those conversations focus on the difficulties that organisations are facing when trying to choose between people or profit in an increasingly CA world. However, the question I'm asking is why are we still choosing when all the evidence tells us we can (and should) have both? This report is recommended for progressive professionals who have the ambition of both striking this balance and avoiding the risks of failing to do so as employee & customer expectations & demands shift".

Bobbi Hartshorne

Founder and Chief
Wellbeing Officer
(CWO), WellWise

 https://www.linkedin.com/in/bobbihartshorne/

"This extremely thorough and interesting report compiled by MBM provides fascinating insights into the values demonstrated by different organisations and the changing focus from profit to people. The authors of this report have shown great imagination in the tools they have used to assess organisational priorities. In this post-covid era, employee wellbeing has become a significant and topical issue in the workplace. The impact of positive employee wellbeing can be enormous in a whole variety of different ways. However, whilst profit/loss is easy to quantify, measures of employee wellbeing and the impact they have on the productivity of the organisation are far harder to calculate. Ultimately, this societal change in focus is here to stay so it is vital for businesses and organisations to embrace it and invest in employee wellbeing in meaningful ways."

Dr Rebecca Williams MA(Cantab), BM, BCh (Oxon)

GP and Stress Management Consultant

 https://www.linkedin.com/in/williamsstressmanagement/

"This enlightening report sheds new light on the ongoing debate between people and profit. The exploration of sustainability uncovers startling insights, emphasizing a concerning lack of focus from major global companies. Notably, Netflix fails to address sustainability altogether, raising specific concerns about this influential company. The report not only addresses the overarching theme of people versus profit but also highlights crucial issues that major corporations should be actively tackling."

Steve Lister

Sustainability Consultant

 https://www.linkedin.com/in/steve-lister/

Table of Content

Foreword from David Ulrich

in https://www.linkedin.com/in/daveulrichpro/

https://daveulrich.com

Rensis Likert Professor, Ross School of Business, University of Michigan Partner, the RBL Group dou@umich.edu

Words matter. They communicate messages, signal priorities, and shape actions. Decades ago, I came to acknowledge the power of words as an English major intending to go to law school where words shape legislation, regulation, and statutes. I ended up studying organization behavior and quickly learned that words also have enormous impact on how people act and organizations operate.

After writing a number of books -- based on observation, interview, and survey research and practice -- I appreciate even more the impact of ideas that flow from words. I frequently engage with and share my "idea friends" that come from works that shape how to think, act on, and feel about how organizations operate.

Why share my passion for words?

Because Darren's report builds on the power of words to characterize how organizations operate.

First, he recognizes that most organizations serve multiple stakeholders, two of which are profit and people. Leaders can focus attention on one or the other, or both. This social vs. economic paradox lies at the heart of many leadership choices.

Second, instead of using observation, interviews, or surveys to capture how an organization navigates this paradox, he explores words leaders use. Public disclosures (annual reports, speeches, board meeting minutes, training programs, and other documents) disclose an organization's commitment to people vs. profit.

His scoring of the 100 largest firms in terms of market value holds up a mirror on the organization's public commitment to these two issues.

Foreword from David Ulrich

My colleagues and I are particularly excited about this approach since we have invested the last three years creating an information source we call Governance and Guidance for Growth through Human Capability (G3HC). In this work, we partnered with Amazon Web Services and used AI/Natural Language Processing (NLP) to score 5,700 disclosures for 2021 and 2022 based on our human capability framework. We scored score four human capability pathways (in talent, leadership, organization, and HR) and 38 initiatives to provide both benchmarking against industry and SEC average for an overall human capability score and for each pathway.

Overall Scores

Overall scores of ABC Co. and 2022 Comparison Groups (average)

ABC CO.	INDUSTRY	SEC AVERAGE	TOP 10% SEC
6.35	5.60	5.49	8.35

Pathway Scores

	TALENT	ORG	LEADERSHIP	HUMAN RESOURCES
ABC CO.	5.28	8.37	5.85	5.91
INDUSTRY	5.92	5.60	5.13	5.73
SEC AVERAGE	5.48	5.55	5.49	5.48
TOP 10% SEC	8.10	8.34	8.54	8.41

■ = Below Parity (5.0)   ■ = Excellent Score (8.0)

We are also able to show the impact of human capability on financial, employee, and citizenship outcomes.

	BUSINESS RESULTS				
	Employee Performance	Financial Performance		Social citizenship or responsibility	
	Revenue per employee	Cash flow (EBITDA)	Tobin's Q (value to book)	Fraud	Litigiousness
HUMAN CAPABILITY SCORE	R2 = .445	R2 = .261	R2 = .253	R2 = .359	R2 = .484

Note: R2 is a statistic that explains the dependent variable (employee, financial, and social citizenship) by the score on the independent variable (Human Capability score).

Given this work, I hope you can see why this report is so exciting. It offers a very innovative way to track an organization's declared commitment to both people and profit and it helps business leaders know how to better use words to communicate, signal, and shape agendas that matter to them, and to other stakeholders.

Executive Summary

Did you know that out of the top 100 global companies, 86 companies mention profit-focused words than people-focused words?

Our extensive and interrogative analysis of corporate annual reports reveals telling data about companies' focus and ethos. This report delves deep into key indicators, such as the frequency of terms like 'wellbeing', 'learning', 'people', and 'profit' to gauge these factors.

Surprisingly, tech companies SAP SE and Reliance Industries are amongst the top five for highest mentions of 'wellbeing', outpacing healthcare giants like Johnson & Johnson. This possibly highlights that newer tech companies are fostering certain people-focused values compared to established entities in people-centric sectors. In contrast, an alarming 34 out of the top 100 companies do not mention 'wellbeing' at all in their annual reports. With the world taking a drastic turn towards employee wellbeing and personal happiness in recent years, these shocking statistics raise questions, and signal where improvement is absolutely crucial.

On the front of intellectual development, companies like Reliance Industries and Tata Consultancy lead in mentions of the word 'learning'. Interestingly, these two companies also showed a high frequency of 'wellbeing', suggesting a multi-dimensional focus on human capital.

Our findings will raise eyebrows in terms of 'People to Profit' ratios. For example, Samsung's high people-to-profit ratio of 1: 7.1 (meaning they have over 7 profit mentions for every people mention) starkly contrasts Sony's lower ratio of 1: 0.7 (meaning they have less than 1 profit mention for every people mention). This may indicate differing priorities or reporting strategies between two companies in the same sector.

Ultimately, this report underscores the need for companies to absolutely ensure that their annual report reflects their company culture, ethos, and focus. Plus, if the annual report does reflect these things, then some companies have a need to improve their culture, ethos, and focus, because if the balance between profit and people focus is not carefully maintained then one will be forsaken for the other.

The data presented here offers a lens to scrutinise these complex documents. Also, it generates thoughtful questions about corporate values, priorities and focus.

Using these metrics as a roadmap, stakeholders can hold companies accountable and make informed decisions. We hope this report serves as a valuable resource for investors, future employees, and the general public interested in understanding the not-so-obvious layers of corporate priorities.

#peoplevsprofit

Introduction

The past few years have seen a tremendous shift in how companies approach employee happiness. On the one hand, we see more and more companies focusing on ensuring their employees feel well, fulfilled, and happy while working. On the other hand, we are also seeing an increasing number of companies pushing back against this idea. Namely, by supporting that profits should come first, and that employees should be focused on their development within the company instead of the benefits they can receive. And yet, the research shows that the happier the employee, the more productive the company, and the better their performance.

As a soft skills training provider determined to change behaviours to help people to be the best version of themselves, we have trained thousands of people to achieve the skills needed to perform better – from negotiation to influencing skills. We have done so for over twenty years. As a result, we have become increasingly intrigued by the language people use.

What kind of language do different kinds of companies use? How does the language differ from one company to the next?

Also, how does this language showcase the kind of values that these companies have? Plus, what can we learn from this?

Please let me tell you a personal story that exemplifies the power of words. When I was seven, my father told me 'Don't run' as we unloaded the weekly food shop from the car to the house. I was keen to help, as any little boy assisting his Dad would be. So, I stood at the car's boot, eagerly waiting to be given something else to take into the house. My father then handed me a one-litre glass jar of orange juice – I think I may have single-handedly been responsible for the move to cartons – and I took off.

Twenty seconds later, I was sprawled out on the concrete path, crying, with blood everywhere. Of course, I had to run. The next six hours that we sat in A&E were spent with my Dad repeatedly telling me that he told me not to run. So, why did I? The answer is in the meaning we give to the words we hear.

I was a seven-year-old boy, so running was always on my mind. At school, we'd have running races, and then we would be running throughout our break times. During P.E. lessons, we ran too, and then, I would run home. That's all that was on my mind. It was like I had just discovered my legs for the first time! (The scene when Forrest Gump gets the leg braces off springs to mind). So, I was running, everywhere, and all the time, and I was trying to beat everyone else's records.

So, my reticular filter was open to 'run'. You may know the reticular filter: when someone mentions a car, or you are looking to buy a particular car, you start seeing that car everywhere. So, I hadn't heard 'don't run', I had only heard 'run'. The power word my Dad had used was 'run' – at least, it was a power word to me. He, on the other hand, was completely oblivious.

'You tend to find evidence of what you believe'.

- Gregg Braden, on the Reticular Activating System

At work, we use power words too. For example, you may say, 'Our company is a long way from making a loss'. The meaning of the sentence is that the company is not near a loss, but the main keyword they hear is 'loss'. Loss is the main thought that people focus on. So, as a result, they are now thinking about the company making a loss. However, if this sentence was structured as 'Our profits could be healthier', the idea you're left with is a more positive one surrounding, 'healthier profits'.

Whenever I speak with a regular client, I know the types of words they'll use a lot. One client is budget focused and the words they'll use will be 'budget', 'cost', and 'discount'. Another client is very future proof in their thinking, and they'll talk about permanently changing behaviours, or what it will look like in the future or how we can sustain it.

As teams and as businesses, people have a vocabulary that is used more in their company than in others. After all company culture is only 'what is said and what is done around here'. By simply being immersed in the company; reading those company emails, sitting in those company meetings and discussing the company with those company employees, words permeate into what we say and become a natural part of our conversation. A company's annual accounts are then a mirror of what we say around here.

Now, whilst we could not scoop up everything ever said within a company; in a meeting, emailed or discussed and then create a word cloud (of course, that would have been fascinating!) we searched for the next best thing, which is the following: companies' annual accounts. A company's leader represents the company the most, and where is a better place than when they speak to their shareholders?

These public accounts are, in a way, spoken by the leaders to the world. So, would it not be interesting to analyse and understand their language? If customers run through the DNA of the company, then the language oozes out of the annual accounts. Similarly, if the company is hell-bent on making a buck, that will ooze through too.

In everyday life, we tell people what we mean through the words we choose. If only we listened to them on a deeper level – oh wait, we did!

Let's look at what companies actually think, beyond the greenwashing and advertising that furthers their agenda, and the marketing strategies that may try to make them appear employee-centred (when they don't all seem to be!). For example, you might be surprised to hear that Royal Dutch Shell – or 'big oil' – is amongst the top companies regarding the people vs profit ratio, with a ratio of **1: 0.9**. That's right, big oil is really concerned about its people. Surprising, isn't it? Maybe.

Excuse the interruption….

If you'd like you or your team to be coached on any of the below, then our Executive Coaching Training Course is for you!

- Category Skills to identify opportunities, sell those opportunities, and deliver those opportunities.

- Build a Joint Business Plan that is well thought through, role-play the delivery, and win more business.

- Become a more effective Account Manager by leaping ahead using our experience.

- Understand the Category better, from the Shopper, Preparer, and Eaters' point of view.

- Lead your team more effectively to achieve your KRAs and become a better coach.

- Present more effectively by sharing a story and engaging the audience with your message much better.

- Assess your Time Management capability so that you can become a more efficient Time Manager.

Our Research Method

How Did We Evaluate Whether a Company is People Focused or Profit Focused?

We are keen to look at the topical issue of people vs Profit in a new light, hence the use of annual reports.

This report took us +500 people hours and 18 months to complete, so safe to say we've given it all we've got!

But how did we do it? Firstly, we used PWC's ranking of the top 100 companies in the world by market capitalisation. We then found the companies' public 2021 annual accounts online and took a peek. Were they primarily people-focused, or primarily focused on making a profit? To take a look at the complete list of the top 100 gathered by PWC, click on the image below.

Rank	Company name	Location	Sector	31 March 2021		31 March 2020	
				Rank +/- (VS Mar 2020)	Market capitalisation ($bn)	Rank	Market capitalisation ($bn)
1	APPLE INC	United States	Technology	2	2,051	3	1,113
2	SAUDI ARAMCO	Saudi Arabia	Energy	-1	1,920	1	1,602
3	MICROSOFT CORP	United States	Technology	-1	1,778	2	1,200
4	AMAZON.COM INC	United States	Consumer Discretionary	0	1,558	4	971
5	ALPHABET INC	United States	Technology	0	1,393	5	799
6	FACEBOOK INC	United States	Technology	1	839	7	475
7	TENCENT	China	Technology	1	753	8	469
8	TESLA INC	United States	Consumer Discretionary	75	641	83	96
9	ALIBABA GRP	China	Consumer Discretionary	-3	615	6	522
10	BERKSHIRE HATHAWAY	United States	Financials	-1	588	9	443
11	TSMC	Taiwan	Technology	9	534	20	235
12	VISA INC	United States	Industrials	0	468	12	316
13	JPMORGAN CHASE	United States	Financials	2	465	15	277
14	JOHNSON & JOHNSON	United States	Health Care	-4	433	10	346
15	SAMSUNG ELECTRONICS	South Korea	Technology	6	431	21	234
16	KWEICHOW MOUTA	China	Consumer Staples	12	385	28	197
17	WALMART INC	United States	Consumer Discretionary	-6	383	11	322
18	MASTERCARD INC	United States	Industrials	0	354	18	243
19	UNITEDHEALTH GRP	United States	Health Care	0	352	19	237
20	LVMH MOET HENNESSY	France	Consumer Discretionary	12	337	32	188

Image courtesy of PWC

We established where their focus was by grouping words into two categories: people and profit. Specifically, we counted the number of times words were mentioned, namely:

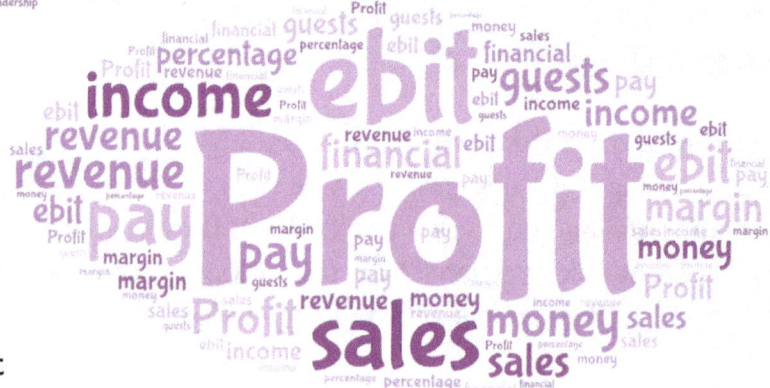

What's your guess? A bank might mention profit much more than people. At the same time, a healthcare company is much more likely to focus on people… But do they? You might be surprised. Let's see...

Psst!

We also added a couple of sneaky sub-categories - learning words and wellbeing. Learning words include:

- ✔ Training
- ✔ Coaching
- ✔ Education
- ✔ Learning
- ✔ Leadership

Stickiest Learning

These are both a sub-category of people-oriented words, and they gave some interesting insights, which we discuss later in the report. Keep an eye out!

Ratio Explanation

Step 1: We counted how many times each of the profit words and people words were mentioned in each annual report.

For example, we searched the Pfizer 2021 annual report for the word 'people' and it returned 57 results.

Step 2: We used the people-oriented words as the constant in this ratio – the people-oriented words are always represented by '1'.

For example, Pfzier's ratio is **1: 0.4**, which shows that they have over double the people mentions than they do profit mentions.

Step 3: Then, the profit-oriented words are measured against the people-oriented words. The people-oriented words are represented with the '1', the profit-oriented words are represented with the ratio to the right of the '1'.

For example, **1: 7.1**. This is Samsung's ratio and shows that they are very profit focused as they mention profit words 7 times more than people words.

Step 4: We used these people versus profit ratios to rank the companies 1-100, with #1 being the most people-focused ratio (Roche Holdings, with a ratio of **1: 0.3**) and #100 being the least people-focused ratio (Samsung, with a ratio of **1: 7.1**).

Take a look at our league table in a few pages time to get the full picture.

Image courtesy of Mark Pinder.

The image below shows a screenshot from Roche Holdings' 2021 annual report, to explain exactly how we counted the people and profit words. 'Employee' was one of our people words, and we can see this highlighted in Roche's report.

At Roche, we believe that integrity is the basis of a sustainable and successful business. We start with ourselves: Every employee has the responsibility to behave with integrity and in accordance with our shared company values and compliance guidelines. Because our commitment is also reflected in the expectations we place on our partners around the world, we require our distributors, suppliers and service providers to meet our integrity standards. We emphasise sustainability and expect our business partners to help foster social and economic development in the communities in which they operate.

We also continue to focus our efforts on our stakeholders' understanding of – and trust in – our organisation. To help ensure that trust, we remain independent of any political affiliation. In 2021, we spent CHF 10.6 million in Switzerland. That spending included payments to industry associations and various chambers of commerce,

to further strengthen our shared ethical mindset across the organisation.

Fostering collaboration through a OneRoche approach

Although we have several distinct businesses and partners within the Roche Group, we know that fostering collaboration through a OneRoche approach is key to our overall success. This approach was the driving force behind many of our compliance and risk and opportunity management efforts in 2021.

One example of this was an initiative aimed at enhancing effectiveness and collaboration across our assurance functions including, but not limited to, compliance, quality, safety, health and environment. The insights of this comprehensive and collaborative gap analysis revealed a high level of competence in many key areas. Moving forward, we see a great opportunity to continue fostering collaboration

Image taken from page 121 of Roche's 2021 annual report.

As a reminder, below are the words we were searching for in the reports:

People Words	Profit Words
People	EBIT
Employee	Sales
Colleague	Profit
Shopper	Income
Guest	Revenue
Customer	

How is This Report Structured?

This report aims to make the large amount of data we have collected much easier to grasp and understand. To this end, we have created eight main sections.

1. In the first section that you've just read, we gave you a brief overview of how we achieved this report.

2. In this current section, we will let you know what you can expect in this report, and whether the annual reports mirror their other outward communication.

3. The third section is our people versus profit ratio league table, in which we pull out many interesting insights.

4. Section number four explores why the idea of 'people vs profit' actually matters. We will be exploring how much has changed since Covid-19, and what being a 'people-focused' company entails in 2023.

5. In this section, we look at individual company insights, and dive deeper into the annual accounts of seven of our one hundred companies.

6. Following this up, is five topic analyses, exploring five important questions when discussing people vs profit:

   - How people focused in your healthcare?

   - Are American banks the hungriest banks?

   - How seriously are the top companies taking our wellbeing?

   - Are these giants green?

   - Do Equality, Diversity and Inclusion make the cut?

7. Then, we have seven global comparisons. Taking two similar companies, we compare their people vs profit mentions, and how this may affect their standing on the global stage, and whether their annual report matches their other outward communication.

8. Finally, we look at how learning and development fits into the annual reports (we couldn't not, being a Learning and Development company ourselves!).

Keep in mind that the results outlined in this report were only collected from 100 companies, meaning that they are not necessarily representative of all companies in their field.

How Do Annual Reports Mirror the Company's Culture?

Much like how we all have our own tone that we add to our emails, companies do this with their annual reports to mirror their company's culture. A key example of this is something that we discuss further on in this report; Amazon's lack of people focus. They have a reputation of being mechanical in their inner workings and having an 'increasingly fractious relationship with (their) workforce', which hasn't made them a fan-favourite with employees.

A recent article described how Amazon workers are 'taught to tear apart each other's ideas' and simply 'climb the wall (when they run into it', which indicates a company culture of unhealthy competition and unfeeling behaviour. The article includes a quote from an exworker who said that 'Nearly every person (she) worked with, she saw cry at their desks'.

This only furthers the robotic culture clearly at large inside Amazon. A culture which is supported by their annual report which features a distinct lack of 'people' words.

Image courtesy of People's Dispatch.

What Do Shareholder Letters Tell Us About a Company's People or Profit Focus?

One of the ways in which we can find out more about whether a company's focus is people or profit is by using their Chairman's or Shareholder's letter. To support this point, we chose the top 3 and bottom 3 ranking companies in terms of our people to profit ratio league table and analysed their shareholder letters. We looked at whether they even have a letter in their annual report and what kind of lexis is used in the letter. We've highlighted our findings alongside a screenshot of the mentioned letter, and then shared our insights with you.

Roche Holdings

Roche

Dear Shareholders

Since its founding 125 years ago, Roche has worked to improve the health and lives of countless people all over the world. Our anniversary year was no exception: In 2021 our more than 100,000 employees and our partners developed, manufactured and provided global access to state-of-the-art diagnostics and treatments for serious diseases including COVID-19. These efforts were guided by the pioneering spirit that has characterised Roche since its founding. My sincere thanks for this.

The COVID-19 pandemic has dominated world events for the past two years or so. It is not the first time that known or yet unknown pathogens have suddenly spread and presented us all with major challenges, and it certainly will not be the last. Roche itself was established under the effect of a pandemic: Fritz Hoffmann had just taken up a position as a merchant in Hamburg in the summer of 1892 when cholera broke out. As a result of this experience, he decided to set up an industrial pharmaceutical company on his return to Basel. His aim was to provide large quantities of effective medicines of uniform quality; this was still a revolutionary concept at the time.

Further milestones in our company's history include our early adoption of biotechnology at a time when almost nobody believed in it. We used the discovery of monoclonal antibodies to revolutionise cancer therapy. With our PCR technology, we were also pioneers in molecular diagnostics.

For Roche, innovation has always been about identifying and seizing opportunities. This will remain so in the future as well. Digitalisation has substantially increased the pace of our company's transformation since I became Chairman of the Board of Directors. We view health data from medical practice as an opportunity to pursue the ongoing development of personalised, and thus even more effective, medicine. At the same time, our analysis of these data supports laboratory research and the development of new clinical trial concepts; it enables us to accelerate approval procedures for innovative therapies and make them available to patients faster.

Going forward, we want to use digitalisation to achieve more medical progress at lower cost. We will therefore once again increase our investment in research and development, even though our

Image taken from page 13 of Roche's 2021 annual report.

Uses 'people' 'lives' and 'health' in the first sentence.

'My sincere thanks' – personal gratitude.

'I would like to thank you' – bringing it to a personal level.

Our first insight is that our people versus profit top spot holder, Roche Holdings, continues their people-focused theme by penning a heartfelt Shareholder's letter. They use the words 'people', 'lives' and 'health', in the first sentence, setting the tone with a lexis centered around people.

The Chairman then adds in his personal gratitude by using the phrases, 'my sincere thanks' and 'I would like to thank you'. By using 'I', the Chairman is bringing a large-scale company down to a much more personal level, and making the reader feel seen. Equally, 'sincere' adds a more genuine tone that moves the report away from sales and profits and towards the people that enable the company to function.

Coca-Cola

Chairman's & CEO's Message

James Quincey
Chairman and CEO

Throughout our company's rich, 136-year history, we've seen many changes and overcome times of uncertainty. Our system's strength and resilience have helped us adapt while remaining true to our purpose: to refresh the world and make a difference.

Our people worked with great dedication in 2021 to help our company emerge stronger from the pandemic and position ourselves for continued growth in 2022 and beyond. We made important decisions about streamlining our brand portfolio; changing the way we work as an organization; and tailoring our investments to target the most promising products and priorities. Through all of the challenges, initiatives and successes of 2021, our environmental, social and governance priorities continued to be embedded in our business and the way we work.

An Integrated Business

Our environmental, social and governance (ESG) priorities are integrated into our strategy. We're focused on areas where we can have a measurable, positive impact on the communities we serve around the world.

Our ESG initiatives are interconnected, and so are the solutions we support. We seek an exponentially greater impact by fostering collective action: partnering across industry, government and society to address shared challenges.

Water is a top business priority. It is the principal ingredient in the products we make and is critical for the agricultural products we use. Through the 2030 Water Security Strategy we announced in 2021, we're focused on achieving water security where the company operates and sources ingredients, concentrating on water-stressed areas—while maintaining 100% replenishment globally.

In 2021, we returned 167% of the water used in our finished beverages to nature and communities. Since 2010, our water, sanitation and hygiene programs have reached more than 18.5 million people globally.

We also continue to make meaningful progress on our World Without Waste packaging initiative. We're continuing to invest in partnerships with innovators and NGOs like our PlantBottle™ partners, World Wildlife Fund and The Ocean Cleanup. We've also set new targets, including a virgin plastic reduction goal and an industry-leading goal to significantly boost our use of reusable packaging.

By 2030, the company aims to have at least 25% of volume globally across our portfolio of brands sold in refillable/returnable glass or plastic bottles, or in refillable containers through traditional fountain or Coca-Cola Freestyle dispensers. We believe that increasing the Coca-Cola system's usage of refillable/returnable containers creates value for customers and consumers, drives increased package collection and simultaneously reduces our carbon footprint.

Water risks and packaging waste are closely linked to climate change. We're reducing our carbon footprint through an intertwined and holistic approach across our ESG priorities. Our vision is for packaging to be reused and recycled as part of a circular economy—which means a world with dramatically lower carbon emissions and climate impacts.

Combating the climate crisis requires a global effort, which is why we worked with experts to set science-based targets. In 2021, we announced that we made solid progress to decarbonize our system by achieving our "drink in your hand" goal. We've increased our ambitions through our 2030 greenhouse gas emissions target to reduce absolute emissions by 25%, and our long-term ambition is to be net zero carbon by 2050.

In 2021, we took action to create a better shared future through investments in economic empowerment; diversity, equity and inclusion (DEI); and giving through The Coca-Cola Foundation. We've refreshed the company's global DEI strategy to reflect the need for greater global reach, broader impact and a focus on equity and economic empowerment.

Image taken from page 3 of Coca-Cola's 2021 annual report.

'Our people' 'together' – evokes a sense of closeness.

'Climate change' 'Water risks' 'Packaging waste' – combating wider issues.

The first thing to note about Coca-Cola's Chairman's letter is that it starts with a smiling and candid photo of the CEO. This sets it aside from other letters where photos of the CEO are included, but they are more formal, in a tie, with a more serious expression. Coca-Cola's use of this more relaxed photo makes James Quincey seem more attainable as Coca-Cola's CEO and Chairman and brings him to a more relatable level.

Throughout their Chairman's letter, Coca-Cola addresses many wider issues; 'climate change', 'water risks' and 'packaging waste'. Use of these phrases highlights an element of care for issues larger than themselves, and also show a practicality in what they are doing to use their power to help combat these issues.

EXXON

> **LETTER TO SHAREHOLDERS**
>
> At ExxonMobil, we are optimistic for the future, confident that our focus on developing and deploying high-value solutions will lead to real progress in meeting the world's economic and environmental challenges. Leveraging our competitive advantages, we're well positioned to meet needs of communities around the world, advance lower-emission solutions, and importantly, reward our shareholders.

Image taken from page 1 of EXXON's 2021 annual report.

'Developing and deploying solutions' – mechanical, and profit-focused.

'Economic and environmental challenges' – not people

'Thank you for investing in our company' – 'invest' suggests economic.

Next, we must turn our attention to EXXON, who are very low ranking in terms of people to profit ratio (**1: 6: 2**). Now, we must give points to EXXON for including a letter when two out of the six companies that we chose didn't include one (Samsung and Kweichow Moutai). However, their letter still highlights a very strong profit focus.

In the first sentence, EXXON uses the phrase 'developing and deploying solutions', which indicates a slant towards the results and 'solutions' rather than the people. Similarly, the final sentence reads 'thank you for investing in our company'. Now whilst we praised Roche for their gratitude, EXXON choses the word 'investing' which removes the personal touch, and re-focuses on the financials, and the shareholders rather than the employees or customers.

Pfizer

A picture of the CEO – adds a personal touch.

To Our Shareholders

2021 was a watershed year for Pfizer. A year in which we set all-time highs in all major areas of focus for our company.

- We reached an estimated 1.4 billion patients with our medicines and vaccines. That's roughly one out of every six people on Earth. Never before has Pfizer's patient impact been so wide-reaching.

- We initiated 13 pivotal clinical studies – the highest number ever for Pfizer.

- We increased our investments in Research & Development (R&D) from $8.9 billion in 2020 to $10.5 billion in 2021.[i]

- And we grew revenues to $81.3 billion (reflecting 92% operational growth), Reported Diluted EPS to $3.85, and Adjusted Diluted EPS to $4.42.[ii]

Paxlovid had received emergency or conditional authorization for use with certain populations in more than 50 countries. We are continuing our discussions with governments and regulators as we endeavor to bring this potential game-changing treatment to patients around the world.

The success of our COVID-19 vaccine and treatment programs has not only made a positive difference in the world; I believe it has fundamentally changed our company and our culture forever. Colleagues across Pfizer are inspired by our achievements and more determined than ever to be part of the next breakthrough. And in a 2021 survey, 95% of our colleagues said they are proud to work for Pfizer, which ranks among the best in corporate America.

Image taken from page 4 of Pfizer's 2021 annual report.

Starts with four facts – leans more towards profit, and less heartfelt.

Uses 'patients' rather than 'people' suggesting they are viewed as something to make profit rather than humans.

Pfizer is an interesting example as they move away from the people-focused status by starting their Chairman's letter with facts and bullet points, which gives a more clinical feel. They use the word 'patients' instead of 'people' which detaches the personal element and suggests a gear towards profit. However, the use of a picture of the CEO in the letter reignites the personal element and makes us remember why they are ranked #2 in people vs profit league table.

Kweichow Moutai & Samsung

The final thing to note from our findings is the absence of a letter from Samsung and Kweichow Moutai's annual reports. This supports their people versus profit ranking as #100 and #98 in the people versus profit ratio league table, because it suggests that they are more focused on the facts and getting the report done, than adding a personal element that would resonate with people.

H.B.D.I (Herrmann Brain Dominance Instrument)

As a further element to understanding what a company's shareholder letter and the wider annual report can show us about that company, we've analysed four companies in terms of HBDI.

Not Sure What HBDI is?

At its core, the HBDI model recognises that each person possesses four distinct thinking quadrants. These quadrants represent different cognitive preferences and thinking styles, ranging from analytical and logical thinking to creative and intuitive approaches. The four quadrants are split into: Red, Yellow, Blue, or Green.

If you want to know more head over to our HBDI Ultimate Guide to find out how understanding the four colours can help you to better understand yourself, and others.

The HBDI model includes a test that deciphers which is your 'dominant' colour. Now it's important to remember that everyone is every colour, in some way. But most of us have a dominant colour for our thinking preference.

A real-life HBDI example of this comes from my wife. Possibly the reddest thinker you will ever meet. When we were viewing houses last year, we walked into a place, and she said she didn't like it. I was baffled, it ticked all of our boxes. She simply said there was a 'feeling'. A classic red signal. Red is the Feeling quadrant, and Red thinkers rely a lot on their gut, and their feelings drive their decisions.

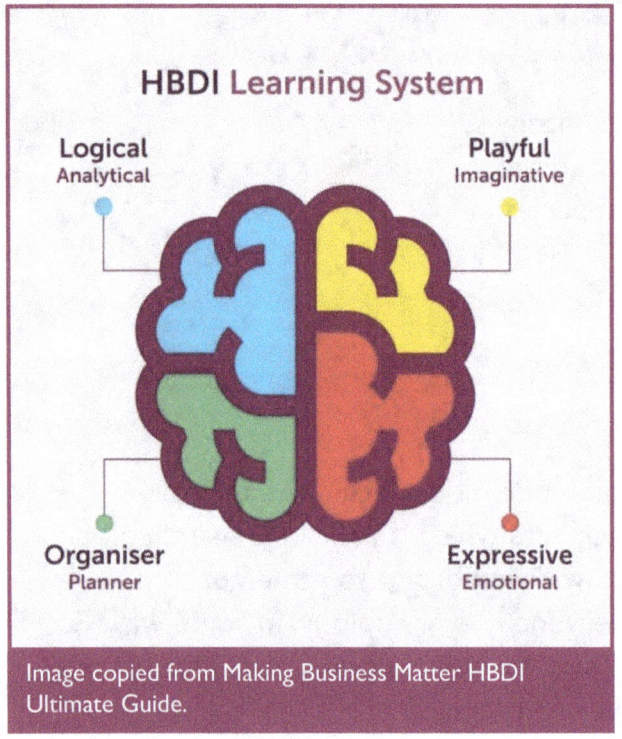

HBDI Learning System

Logical
Analytical

Playful
Imaginative

Organiser
Planner

Expressive
Emotional

Image copied from Making Business Matter HBDI Ultimate Guide.

The four colours can easily be remembered with the four F's: Fact, Form, Feeling, and Future. As you can see below each colour has a different focus, and whilst Blue and Green are more logical and planned, working on the left side of the brain, Red and Yellow are more feeling and emotional, working for the right side of the brain.

The toughest communication is where it is diametrically opposed. In the case of HBDI, that is Yellow to Green and vice versa, and Blue to Red and vice versa. This is because the thinking of the opposite quadrant is so dramatically different to our own quadrant.

Blue	Green	Red	Yellow
Fact = Logical, technical, and financial	**Form =** Organised, detailed, and structured	**Feeling =** Emotional, sensory, and people	**Future =** Risk taker, intuitive, and big picture

Image copied from Making Business Matter HBDI Ultimate Guide.

Whilst we understand that each annual report will have had many different people from the same company working on it, and each of those have a dominant colour, we're looking at the overall colour quadrant that is on display when reading the company's annual report, and therefore how that company's employees may think. You know what it's like when you join a company and start to learn their jargon, start to use their jargon, and then the jargon becomes part of you.

If you're intrigued about your's and your team's HBDI colour, then head over to the MBM Shop to purchase your full HBDI profile. This profile will help you develop insights on how you learn, make decisions, work in teams, solve problems and communicate.

Red Quadrant: Coca-Cola

Firstly, displaying a dominant Red colour, is Coca-Cola. They rank #3 with a people to profit ratio of **1: 0.5**, so it would be safe to assume their annual report has a strong people focus. Their report displays many 'Red' characteristics, which is known as the Relational quadrant. For example, in their shareholder letter they use phrases like 'together' and 'our people', which moves them away from being just a business and towards a familial-like tone.

Throughout the report, Coca-Cola use photos of real people in various countries around the world, and how sustainability and agricultural affects them. The report also addresses issues of climate change and waste. This gives the report a broadness, rather than a narrow focus of just financials. The topics that the report cover highlights the caring nature of the company, and the fact that they are people focused.

Image from page 42 of Coca-Cola's 2021 annual report.

Blue Quadrant: Samsung

SAMSUNG

In contrast, the opposite colour of Blue features heavily in Samsung's report. Throughout the report, there are many tables, numbers, and dates, showing a skew towards facts and statistics. Equally, their omission of a shareholder letter shows a dismissal of the emotional tone that reports like Roche have shown, as Samsung focus on earnings, revenue, and risk management in their report.

[PLP Business]

- Details of acquisition
  In accordance with the resolution of the Board of Directors on April 30, 2019, the Company acquired PLP business from Samsung Electro-Mechanics Co., Ltd.(location: South Korea; CEO: Kyehyun Kyung) at a price of KRW 785,000 million on June 1, 2019 to strengthen its semiconductor competitiveness through securing next-generation packaging technology.

- Details of the above statement can be found in the "Business Acquisition from Related Parties", published in DART (http://dart.fss.or.kr/) on April 30, 2019.

(KRW 100 mil)

	Account	Forecast		Actual			
		1st Year	2nd Year	1st Year		2nd Year	
				Actual	Difference	Actual	Difference
PLP Business	Sales	101	219	-	-	-	-
	Operating Income	-1,273	-2,155	-1,095	14%	-44	98%
	Net Income	-1,273	-2,155	-1,095	14%	-2,146	0%

❖ No third-party sales is recognized from PLP business as its products are internally transferred within the Company's manufacturing process.

❖ Actual operating income and net income for first year of acquisition (seven month period ended December 31, 2019) differs by 14% from the forecast due to several factors such as reduction in wages.

❖ Actual operating income for the second year (the year ended December 31, 2020) of acquisition differs by 98% from the forecast due to several factors such as reduction in wages.

[Corephotonics Ltd.]

- Samsung Electronics Benelux B.V. (SEBN), the Company's subsidiary, acquired 83.9% of the equity shares of Corephotonics Ltd.(location: Tel Aviv, Israel; CEO: David Mendlovic) on January 28, 2019 and additional 8.5% on March 4, 2019 to secure CIS optical technology and talent.

Image from Samsung's 2021 Annual Report.

The lack of colour and pictures throughout the report also shows a lack of the human touch, and instead gives a cold and mechanical feel.

Yellow Quadrant: L'Oréal

L'ORÉAL

Yellow is a colour that features heavily within L'Oréal's annual report. Though it is the shortest of our annual reports, the structure, and the way the pages are laid out creates a creative landscape that supports a beauty brand. Each page includes colour, different layouts, and pictures of diverse women.

Yellow is known as the Experimental quadrant, and people who are dominant in Yellow are usually creative and think long term.

The report talks about sustainability in the future, which highlights bigger picture thinking, alongside the diversity that they display, which shows creative thinking as they outpace many beauty brands.

Image from page 21 of L'Oréal's 2021 annual report.

Green Quadrant: Aramco

The final quadrant that we analysed was Green, and the company that befits this quadrant is Aramco. Within their first ten pages they show a timeline of their history, as seen below, that shows methodological, 'Green' thinking.

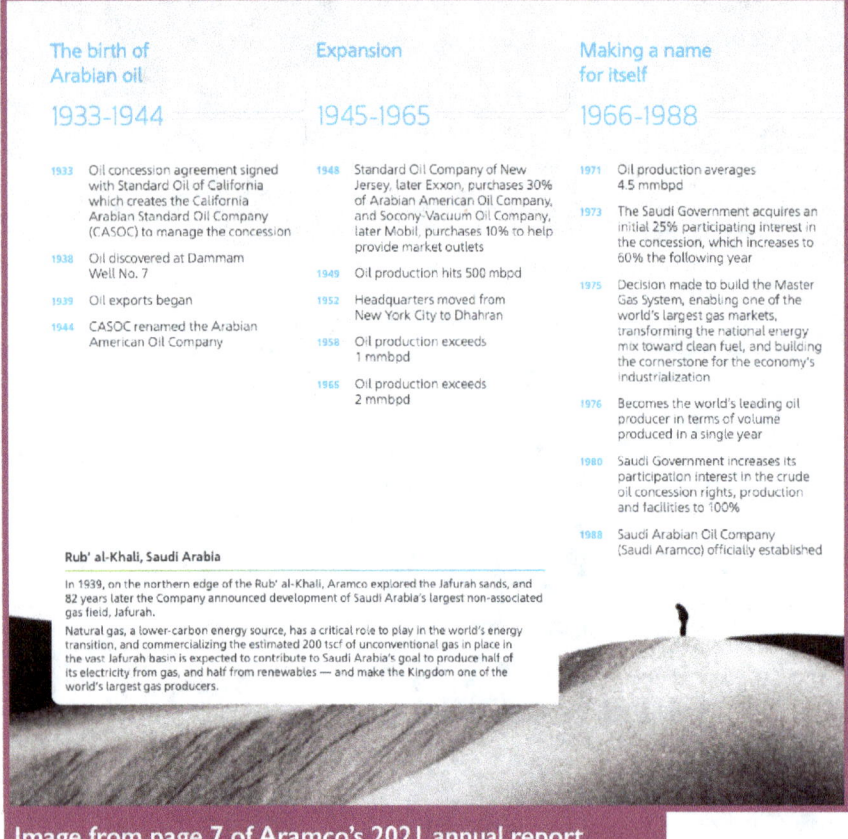

The birth of Arabian oil
1933-1944

1933 Oil concession agreement signed with Standard Oil of California which creates the California Arabian Standard Oil Company (CASOC) to manage the concession

1938 Oil discovered at Dammam Well No. 7

1939 Oil exports began

1944 CASOC renamed the Arabian American Oil Company

Expansion
1945-1965

1948 Standard Oil Company of New Jersey, later Exxon, purchases 30% of Arabian American Oil Company, and Socony-Vacuum Oil Company, later Mobil, purchases 10% to help provide market outlets

1949 Oil production hits 500 mbod

1952 Headquarters moved from New York City to Dhahran

1958 Oil production exceeds 1 mmbpd

1965 Oil production exceeds 2 mmbpd

Making a name for itself
1966-1988

1971 Oil production averages 4.5 mmbpd

1973 The Saudi Government acquires an initial 25% participating interest in the concession, which increases to 60% the following year

1975 Decision made to build the Master Gas System, enabling one of the world's largest gas markets, transforming the national energy mix toward clean fuel, and building the cornerstone for the economy's industrialization

1976 Becomes the world's leading oil producer in terms of volume produced in a single year

1980 Saudi Government increases its participation interest in the crude oil concession rights, production and facilities to 100%

1988 Saudi Arabian Oil Company (Saudi Aramco) officially established

Rub' al-Khali, Saudi Arabia

In 1939, on the northern edge of the Rub' al-Khali, Aramco explored the Jafurah sands, and 82 years later the Company announced development of Saudi Arabia's largest non-associated gas field, Jafurah.

Natural gas, a lower-carbon energy source, has a critical role to play in the world's energy transition, and commercializing the estimated 200 tscf of unconventional gas in place in the vast Jafurah basin is expected to contribute to Saudi Arabia's goal to produce half of its electricity from gas, and half from renewables — and make the Kingdom one of the world's largest gas producers.

Image from page 7 of Aramco's 2021 annual report.

○-○-◉ **Portfolio optimization**

Through portfolio optimization, Aramco seeks to unlock value, enhance its capital structure and reallocate capital to higher growth and return investments. Aramco has a comprehensive and disciplined internal approval process for capital expenditures, new projects and debt issuance. It analyzes future projects based on strategic, operational, commercial, and financial targets. Aramco's unique reserves and resource base, operational flexibility, field management practices, and strong cash flow generation serve as a foundation for its low gearing and flexibility to allocate capital.

Aramco's report is one of the higher word counts at 114,434 words, which suggests that the report is detailed and meticulous. Also, throughout their report the word 'project' is used 99 times. The word project is used a lot by Green thinkers as it implies a timeline, steps and organisation.

My Own Experience of a Colour Company

For 13 years I worked for Sainsbury's. One of the top 4 supermarkets in the UK with current sales of about £31bn. During that time, I re-applied, as most people did, for my job 8 times. Bearing in mind that in my latter days I was managing a one billion pound portfolio of goods, the restructures had a detrimental effect on what we achieved. We could have achieved much more if we weren't looking over our shoulder and hanging onto our jobs.

Sainsbury's got overtaken by what it called, in the early days, that pile it high supermarket – Tesco. In 1995 Tesco took the lead and are now a £58 billion company. Sainsbury's lacked vision and are still lagging behind with initiatives like having to follow Tesco with the equivalent of Clubcard products deals.

In the 90s, Sainsbury's committees, processes, and paperwork was immense. It took a long time to get a decision as they were risk adverse whereas Tesco had a phrase of 'Ready, Fire, Aim', and got things out there quicker and then learnt & improved. Instead, Sainsbury's more operated on a model of 'Ready, Aim, Aim, Aim, Fire'.

Facts were needed and sought. Unfortunately, analysis often became analysis paralysis. Sainsbury's was a Green company, as termed by HBDI. Led by process. Lacking the Red HBDI quadrant (re-applying for my job many times), not having a clear vision - (The Yellow part) - Being overtaken by Tesco, and whilst the Blue offacts were sought, without the vision, coupled with being risk adverse, the facts were analysed with little or no context (Yellow thinking).

Companies can have HBDI colours, as Sainsbury's did in the 90's. These colours can be dictated by the industry. For example, the healthcare market is Red – Feelings and people. Yet, the tech industry is Blue – engineers, until a disruptor comes along, like Apple and applies Yellow thinking – innovation and creativity.

Welcome to the Big League

Whilst the database (see our 'Interested in the Specifics?' page for more details) that we have built over the course of this project has many insights, with each people and profit word broken down into their respective mentions, the table below shows the overall people to profit ratio. The holy grail, if you will.

As a quick reminder the '1' is always representative of the 'people' words, and the decimal that follows represents the 'profit' words. As an example, you can see that the first on our table is Roche Holdings, with a ratio of **1: 0.3**, which shows that 'people' words are mentioned in their annual report approximately 3 times more than 'profit' words.

Company	People to Profit Ratio	People to Profit Ratio Ranking
Roche Holdings	1: 0.3	#1
Pfizer Inc	1: 0.4	#2
Coca-Cola	1: 0.5	#3
ASML Holding NV	1: 0.6	#4
LVMH Moet Hennessy	1: 0.6	#5
JPMorgan Chase	1: 0.7	#6
Bristol-Myer SQB	1: 0.7	#7
Sony Group Corp	1: 0.7	#8
Charter Communications	1: 0.8	#9
PayPal Holdings	1: 0.8	#10
China Merchants Bank	1: 0.8	#11
Royal Dutch Shell	1: 0.9	#12
SAP SE	1: 0.9	#13
T-Mobile US Inc	1: 0.9	#14
Adobe Inc	1: 1.0	#15
Prosus NV	1: 1.1	#16
United Parcel	1: 1.1	#17
Agricultural Bank of China	1: 1.1	#18
Ind & Comm Bank	1: 1.1	#19

Company	People to Profit Ratio	People to Profit Ratio Ranking
Texas Instrument	1: 1.1	#20
Salesforce	1: 1.1	#21
Boeing Co	1: 1.2	#22
Home Depot	1: 1.2	#23
Broadcom Inc	1: 1.2	#24
Intel Corp	1: 1.2	#25
Mastercard Inc	1: 1.2	#26
Cisco Systems	1: 1.2	#27
Verzion Communications	1: 1.2	#28
Tata Consultancy	1: 1.2	#29
UnitedHealth GRP	1: 1.2	#30
Ping AN	1: 1.3	#31
Comcast Corp	1: 1.3	#32
Bank of China	1: 1.3	#33
TSMC	1: 1.3	#34
Lowe's COS Inc	1: 1.3	#35
Reliance INDS	1: 1.3	#36
NVIDIA Corp	1: 1.4	#37
Union Pac Corp	1: 1.4	#38
Thermo Fisher	1: 1.4	#39
Unilever plc	1: 1.4	#40
Amazon	1: 1.5	#41
Abbvie Inc	1: 1.5	#42
Qualcomm Inc	1: 1.5	#43
AIA	1: 1.6	#44
BHP Group Ltd	1: 1.6	#45
Honeywell Intl	1: 1.7	#46
Meituan	1: 1.7	#47
Microsoft Corp	1: 1.7	#48

Company	People to Profit Ratio	People to Profit Ratio Ranking
Oracle Corp	1:1.9	#49
China Mobile	1:1.9	#50
Tencent	1:2.0	#51
Medtronic plc	1:2.0	#52
China Construction Bank	1:2.0	#53
Accenture plc	1:2.1	#54
Pepsico Inc	1:2.1	#55
Volkswagen AG	1:2.2	#56
Procter & Gamble	1:2.2	#57
AT&T Inc	1:2.2	#58
Johnson & Johnson	1:2.3	#59
Wells Fargo & Co	1:2.3	#60
Nike Inc	1:2.3	#61
Apple	1:2.3	#62
Nextera Energy	1:2.3	#63
Tesla Inc	1:2.3	#64
Netflix Inc	1:2.5	#65
Starbucks Corp	1:2.5	#66
Bank of America	1:2.6	#67
Alibaba GRP	1:2.6	#68
Danaher Corp	1:2.6	#69
Berkshire Hathaway	1:2.6	#70
AstraZeneca plc	1:2.7	#71
Linde plc	1:2.7	#72
Anheuser-Busch	1:2.9	#73
Costco Wholesale	1:2.9	#74
Facebook Inc	1:3.0	#75
Novo Nordisk	1:3.0	#76
Merck & Co	1:3.0	#77

Company	People to Profit Ratio	People to Profit Ratio Ranking
Novartis AG	1:3.1	#78
McDonald's	1:3.3	#79
Citigroup Inc	1:3.3	#80
Abbott Labs	1:3.5	#81
Philip Morris Inc	1:3.5	#82
VISA Inc	1:3.6	#83
Siemens	1:3.7	#84
Saudi Aramco	1:3.7	#85
L'Oreal	1:3.8	#86
Walmart Inc	1:3.8	#87
Nestle SA	1:3.9	#88
Wuliangye Yibin	1:3.9	#89
Royal Bank of Canada	1:4.0	#90
Eli Lilly & Co	1:4.1	#91
Alphabet Inc	1:4.4	#92
The Walt Disney Company	1:4.4	#93
Softbank Group	1:4.8	#94
Chevron Corp	1:5.4	#95
Amgen Inc	1:5.6	#96
Toyota Motor	1:5.8	#97
Kweichow Moutai	1:5.8	#98
EXXON Mobil Corp	1:6.2	#99
Samsung Electronics	1:7.1	#100

Insight #1: Unsurprising First and Last Place

We begin our key insights with the obvious, that Roche Holdings are the best in terms of people-focus, and Samsung are the worst. The placing of Roche and Samsung are perhaps expected. The fact that Roche is a pharmaceutical company suggests that it is expected to focus on people more than profit. Samsung, on the other hand, is a technology company expected to do the opposite, and focus on the newest gadget, and therefore the next profit. With the next highest ratio, of **1: 6.2** (EXXON, it seems Samsung is truly the most profit-focused, being +0.9 higher than the next closest company.

Insight #2: A Shocking Percentage

Something quite noticeable when looking at our people vs profit league table is the volume of companies with a ratio over 1. As mentioned in our explanation, anything over a ratio of **1: 1** suggests that the company has more of a profit focus. Our people to profit ratio table shows 85% of companies mentioned profit words more than they mentioned people words. This shockingly high percentage may indicate that most companies today are still focused on profit rather than people, despite seismic shifts in the need for mental health and wellbeing of employees.

Insight #3: Reaching Balance?

The final insight is that almost 10% of companies had a ratio of **1:1** or **1: 1.1** highlighting that several companies are using profit and people words fairly equally. This indicates a more balanced work culture, as companies try to balance their strive for profit with the need to look after their people. Which is good news.

Does People vs Profit Matter?

You might be asking yourself why you even need to read about people vs profit, and why it matters. Well, below we explore just that. Spoiler: the answer to the above question is, quite simply, yes. It does matter. It matters because this post-pandemic world has changed the priorities of employees, and in order to change with the world, we need to know whether companies themselves are changing.

Understanding where a company lies in the people vs profit continuum can help companies (like yours, perhaps!) better navigate their strategic approach. For example, where a people-centric model might help you boost employee morale, find employees who are loyal, and increase your profitability. Other companies, who are mainly focused on bringing in a big profit (profit-centric model), might benefit more from learning how to better their public image (making them more attractive employers), increase their employees' levels of engagement, or grow more continually.

Why are People-Focused Approaches Necessary in 2023?

Over the past few years, we have seen a significant change in how companies approach their care for employees. Specifically, more companies have come forward and shared how they have been struggling to find talent that wants to stick around and are grappling with high turnover rates. This is a problem that many HR specialists have been discussing for years: employees want more.

But gaining more is the surface solution. You see it's not about the quantity, but rather it's about the quality. Having seen death and sickness, the pandemic has awoken an inner revolt in employees. They want better living and working conditions and are no longer willing to work for companies that do not care for their wellbeing or their work-life balance.

Excuse the interruption....

If you're looking to be the best version of yourself, take a look at our training courses.

We have a wide range of training courses, and the below are our most popular:

- ❤ Leadership Skills
- ❤ People Management
- ❤ Teamwork Skills

We can help you move towards a more people-focused company, who in turn, create the profits you're striving for.

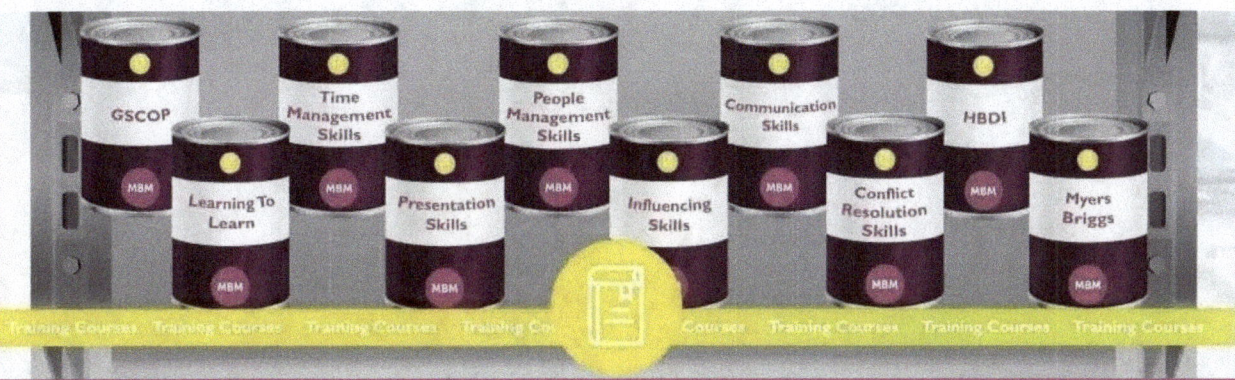

Employees are no longer willing to forego basic respect and proper care simply to receive a few more monthly pounds. Instead, they are willing to take a pay cut, as long as it means that coming to work is something they enjoy.

Employees have graduated to the final levels of Maslow's Hierarchy of Needs. And yet some companies don't seem to have caught up with their needs.

The higher up we go in Maslow's hierarchy of needs, the more engagement is required, and the more feminine leadership thrives. It's like the saying, 'masculine energy builds a house and feminine energy transforms it into a home'. Similarly, a rigid 'profit' system based on masculine leadership is important to build the foundation for survival, but a flowing 'people' focused is based on feminine leadership which is important for expansion. With that in mind, it is no surprise that McKinsey found that companies that prioritise developing their employees have higher profit returns.

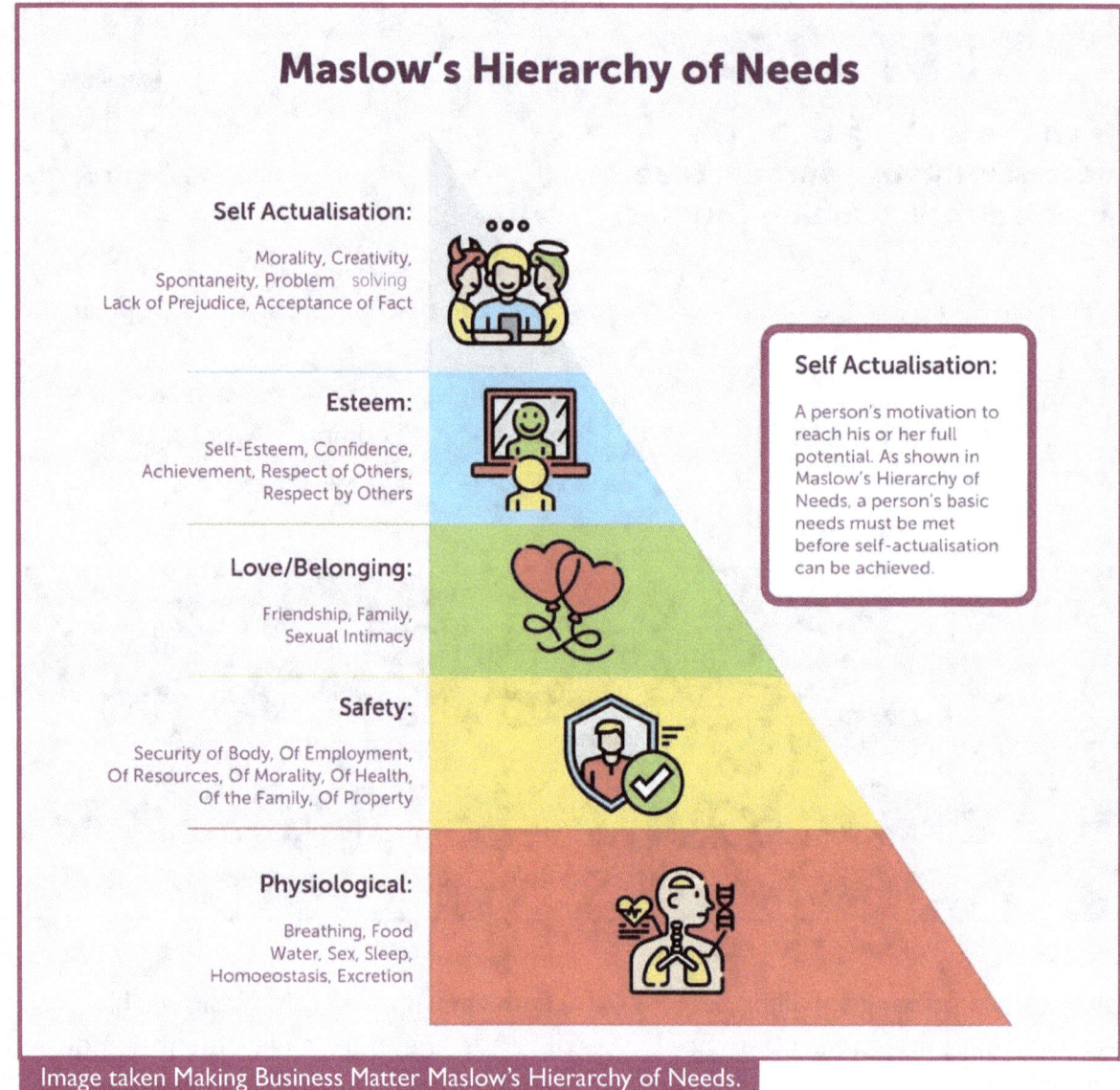

Maslow's Hierarchy of Needs

Self Actualisation:

Morality, Creativity, Spontaneity, Problem solving Lack of Prejudice, Acceptance of Fact

Esteem:

Self-Esteem, Confidence, Achievement, Respect of Others, Respect by Others

Love/Belonging:

Friendship, Family, Sexual Intimacy

Safety:

Security of Body, Of Employment, Of Resources, Of Morality, Of Health, Of the Family, Of Property

Physiological:

Breathing, Food Water, Sex, Sleep, Homoeostasis, Excretion

Self Actualisation:

A person's motivation to reach his or her full potential. As shown in Maslow's Hierarchy of Needs, a person's basic needs must be met before self-actualisation can be achieved.

Image taken Making Business Matter Maslow's Hierarchy of Needs.

So, why is it that some companies seem not to be phased by this change in employee wants at all? Why is it that we still see companies primarily focused on making profits while employee wellbeing comes second? These are important questions to be asking, and they are some we address throughout this section.

What Does Being a People-Focused Company Entail in 2023?

In 2023, companies have two options: to accept that we now live in a day and age where employees have more demands, or to be left behind and struggle to find people willing to work for them. For example, we are already seeing how companies who refuse to offer work from-home opportunities are struggling to keep people engaged, and to keep attracting employees to come work for them. This is not uncommon, as this is a trend, we are seeing both within and outside the UK.

So, what exactly does being a people-focused company entail in 2023? Key themes have been highlighted throughout various reports over the past few years. For example, in its State of the Global Workplace: 2023 Report, Gallup highlights that employee engagement is at an all-time high globally. However, it also highlights that the 'majority of the world's employees are quiet quitting', namely, they are not very engaged. At the same time, over 18% have reported 'loud quitting', which refers to being actively disengaged.

Quiet quitting, as Gallup describes it, is when employees are:

Filling a seat and watching the clock. They put in the minimum effort required, and they are psychologically disconnected from their employer.

- Gallup, 2023, p.4

On the other hand, loud quitting is where:

Employees take actions that directly harm the organisation, undercutting its goals and opposing its leaders. At some point along the way, the trust between employee and employer was severely broken.

- Gallup, 2023, p.4

Interestingly, Gallup has estimated that low engagement, which results in the forms of quitting discussed above, cost the global economy over US $8.8 trillion (GBP £6.9 trillion). At the same time, it accounts for 9% of global GDP. The culprit is clear: low engagement.

Does Prospective Talent Read the Annual Accounts?

In short, the answer is yes. The longer answer is that, even if they're not, they should be, and in this case, this puts even more emphasis on companies' annual reports mirroring or improving their ethos. Eloy Barrantes conducted a study via LinkedIn that shows that 14.5% of the people reading annual reports are students and applicants.

Who are the readers of Annual Reports?

- 25.0% Employees
- 17.0% Analysts
- 14.5% Applicants and students
- 12.1% Retail shareholders
- 31.4% Others

Image courtesy of Eloy Barrantes via LinkedIn.

This data showing that future employees do in fact read the annual reports highlights the need for companies' annual reports to mirror and improve their company culture and ethos. This study also relates back to the trend we noted in which employees are demanding more from their employers since the pandemic. Therefore when looking at an annual report that is heavily profit-focused, they may instead look for a company that has more of an emphasis on the people and their wellbeing.

How Do the Drivers of Engagement Relate?

As Gallup found, low engagement is costing companies billions. So how can companies re-engage employees? Utilise the key drivers of engagement.

First, employees need to have meaningful work. This is work that allows them to enjoy a certain degree of autonomy, and work that involves small and empowered teams. It also involves some time for relaxing as opposed to feeling as though they are extremely limited in terms of free time. It utilises a select-to-fit model whereby individuals are chosen to be part of a team only if they are deemed to be a good fit for the entire team, reducing the risk that someone who is not a good fit comes in and potentially hurts the company culture and team spirit that has been slowly built up.

Second, there is supportive management, which involves clear and transparent goals, coaching, investment in the development of managers, as well as an agile approach to performance management.

Third, a positive work environment is important as well, whereby individuals can work in a flexible work environment within a culture of recognition and have the pleasure to be part of an equal, diverse and inclusive work environment (we take a deeper look at EDI in our topic analyses on page 83). Employees can then enjoy the opportunity to grow as they receive training and support on the job. This also may involve having access to facilitated talent mobility and being self-directed.

Finally, there is trust in leadership. With a clear mission, purpose, continuous investment in people, transparency and honesty, people can be inspired throughout the process. A people focused company, in 2023, must eloquently combine the technological advances that are now expected from a modern company to the established best practices known as engagement 'boosters', as those mentioned above. It is a tricky job, but one that is possible, nonetheless.

Herzberg's Motivators

We couldn't talk about employee engagement without mentioning Frederick Herzberg's Motivators. He proposed that at work we have two sets of needs, which he called: Hygiene Factors and Motivating Factors. The first are factors that won't cause employees to work any harder, but they will cause dissatisfaction if they're not present. The latter encourages employees to work harder and aim higher.

Hygiene Factors:

- Company policies
- Supervision
- Work relationships
- Work conditions
- Remuneration Salary
- Security

Motivating Factors:

- Achievement
- Recognition
- Rewarding work
- Increased responsibility
- Personal advancement
- Growth opportunities

The connection to this report is that the companies who are more profit-focused in their annual report are probably focusing on hygiene factors only, and need to utilise strategies that implement motivating factors.

"This report by MBM is a fascinating read for all of us who are passionate about the value of human capital. I really hope this eye-opening read makes leaders sit up and take notice!" - **Kate Cousens, Co-Founder DICE Business**

Highly Engaged Employees?

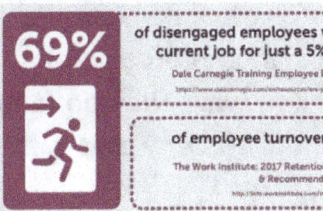

69% of disengaged employees would leave their current job for just a 5% pay increase.
Dale Carnegie Training Employee Engagement Study
https://www.dalecarnegie.com/en/resources/are-your-employees-motivated

of employee turnover are preventable.
The Work Institute: 2017 Retention Report: Trends, Reasons & Recommendations
http://info.workinstitute.com/retentionreport2017

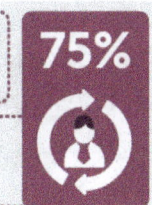 **75%**

Disengaged workers cause losses in productivity between **$450 & $500 BILLION A YEAR**
Mental Health America: Mind the Workplace

Excuse the interruption....

After all the talk about employee engagement, we thought this handy infographic might help you understand a bit more the possible benefits and downfalls of having, and not having, engaged employees.

For the high-resolution version of this infographic, simply click on the image.

Still want to know more?

There's plenty more where that came from:

- The Employee Engagement Equation
- Employee Engagement Course
- Book Review: Employee Engagement

Actively disengaged employees are almost twice as likely as engaged employees to seek new jobs.
Gallup: The Relationship Between Engagement at Work and Organizational Outcomes, 2016 | State of the American Workplace, 2017

20% MORE SALES

21% MORE PROFITABLE

51% OF THE US WORKFORCE IS NOT ENGAGED / IS ACTIVELY LOOKING FOR A NEW JOB OR WATCHING FOR OPENINGS

59% LESS TURNOVER RATE FOR LOW TURNOVER COMPANIES (THOSE WITH MORE THAN 40% ANNUALIZED TURNOVER)

24% LESS TURNOVER RATE FOR HIGH TURNOVER COMPANIES (THOSE WITH 45% OR LOWER ANNUALIZED TURNOVER)

17% HIGHER PRODUCTIVITY

10% MORE CUSTOMER LOYALTY/ ENGAGEMENT (LIKELIHOOD TO RECOMMEND, REPEAT BUSINESS)

28% LESS SHRINKAGE

41% REDUCED ABSENTEEISM

70% FEWER SAFETY INCIDENTS

engaged employees are **2.1x more** successful in work performance

A High Number of People Words Means a Company is People Focused...Or Does it?

We need to clarify that when we draw upon the 'people' vs 'profit' dichotomy, we are not insinuating that companies focused on people completely disregard profits, nor do profit oriented companies 'not care' about their people. Rather, it's an exploration of where their primary focus lies and how that shapes what they say and what they do (and how this may or may not be a common occurrence in this field, and if so, why that is the case?).

There can be varied interpretations of what constitutes a 'people' company or a 'profit' company, but we will discuss how we see this further below. Often, the terminology is gauged through a company's communications: their reports, mission statements, or public announcements. For example, a high incidence of 'people' related keywords might suggest a company leans towards a people-focused approach. However, it's important to underscore that keyword ratios alone do not provide an absolute measure; they merely offer an indicative lens.

The first question you may ask yourself is 'Since you looked at annual accounts, it makes sense that profits are more discussed than people. Does that mean that a company is profit focused?'. Indeed, this is a good question to be asking. Our access to quality information is limited to the information that is made public.

Likewise, it would be useless to look at published documents that specifically address profits (like a Q3 financial statement) or people (like a diversity report), as the point is to explore whether a company is indeed people-focused or whether it's true focus is on the profit it is making. We believe that annual reports are a good combination of financial voice, leadership and a lens to company culture.

Similarly, we need to mention that while a high number of people' keywords may indicate a company that is highly focused on making its people happy and keeping its workforce engaged, this is not an absolutely irrefutable claim. Some companies may focus more on their people this year, while they may change this completely in future years.

How Has Covid-19 Affected the Skew on People vs Profit?

Employee satisfaction has changed since Covid-19. Whereas employee satisfaction was primarily based on employee benefits before the pandemic, this has expanded to more complex requirements. For example, a Harvard Business Review study has shown that nowadays, employees have high expectations of their employers. In fact, 65% said they would rather accept lower pay than a negative work environment.

Today's employees are much more likely to take a great working environment over one that offers higher pay but a terrible culture. Similarly, the review suggested that not only do employees have high expectations, but they especially 'care about whether companies foster environments where employees can be themselves (47%) and have a positive impact on society (46%)' as employees want to 'know that they're making a difference within their companies'.

At its core, employee satisfaction now encompasses aspects like work environment, job content, work-life balance, remuneration, growth opportunities, and recognition, but this is especially enhanced through a company's ability to allow 'post-Covid-friendly' options, such as the ability to work from home, and more flexible hours.

Did You Know?

Between December 2019 and March 2022, the number of people working from home in the UK increased from 4.7 million to 9.9 million. The number of homeworkers increased by more than 50% across all UK regions.

We have seen how Covid-19 has changed the world of work, with companies calling it the Future of Work, the Digitalisation, and referring to current trends in the labour market such as the Great Resignation as key transformative occurrences that will change how we work forever. The Future of Work, accelerated by digitalisation, has completely reshaped the work sphere, making flexibility and autonomy normal parts of daily life within the work sphere (or at least, it has made it a desirable aspect of most positions!).

The Great Resignation phenomenon, which is where numerous people have purposely left their jobs in search of better opportunities or lifestyle changes (e.g. access to more benefits, better flexible hours, etc) has made employee satisfaction extremely important. It is no longer a peripheral concept; it's now a decisive factor in staff retention strategies, and it must be considered for workplaces to be seen as attractive to work at.

Indeed, Gen-Z (born 1997-2012) is coming onto the market and changing the game – they are unlikely to accept working circumstances that do not minimally match what they want and working conditions that do not fit their basic standards. They are making the world of work much more colloquial, whereby employers are treated more as friends than as 'big bosses'.

This new culture will have a tremendous effect on the way hiring processes are taking place, largely because the more Gen-Z requires from employers, the more employers will have to comply to avoid completely losing its workforce. Covid-19 has forced companies to move their focus from profits to people, for fear that they will be left behind in this shifting space.

Excuse the interruption....

As mentioned above, the increase in working from home and hybrid working is perhaps the biggest change that Covid-19 brought about, and we know working from home is not always as easy as it might seem.

We've developed this handy infographic to help you work from home effectively. Simply click on the image below to view the full high-resolution version.

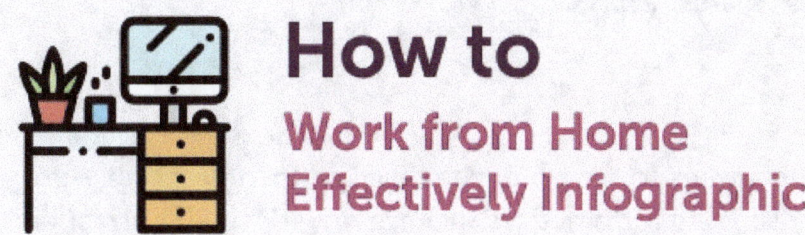

Is Working from Home a Good Idea?

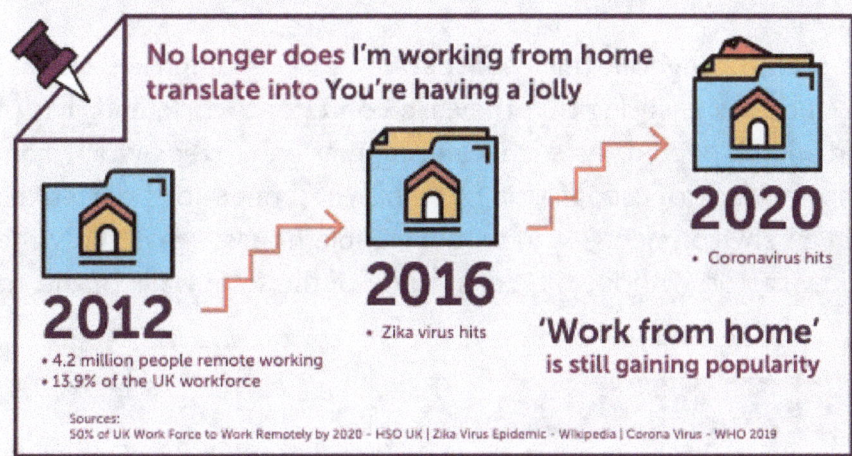

No longer does I'm working from home translate into You're having a jolly

2012
- 4.2 million people remote working
- 13.9% of the UK workforce

2016
- Zika virus hits

2020
- Coronavirus hits

'Work from home' is still gaining popularity

Sources:
50% of UK Work Force to Work Remotely by 2020 - HSO UK | Zika Virus Epidemic - Wikipedia | Corona Virus - WHO 2019

M.I.N.D.S.E.T Adopt 7 Best Practices

Read the full Work from Home article. Just search 'work from home mbm'.

How can I Work from home Myself?

(Bonus: this helpful infographic has many friends on our Infographics page).

Individual Company Insights

Insight #1: Tesla

Tesla Inc, led by Elon Musk, is an example of a company whose People to Profit ratio is representative of some of the company values that we hear Tesla being associated with. With only 257 mentions of people, compared to 601 of profit, we could deem the company a profit-minded one, something that is transpiring in Musk's latest approach to work-from-home schemes.

Musk told his employees to return to the office or to 'pretend to work elsewhere', showcasing his disregard for practices that are now deemed normal, and even expected, from employers.

Yet, as we have seen throughout this report so far, placing emphasis on employees' satisfaction now includes ensuring that they are content at work, and that their wellbeing is acknowledged and respected. As such, refusing that employees work from home, in 2023, indeed shows a lack of recognition of employees' need for policies that enable them to work in an environment – and within flexible hours – that allow them to be as productive as they can be without the constraints of the four walls of the company.

Excuse the interruption....

Did you know we also offer branded coaching cards? Every line manager needs a little help to coach. A pack of company cards with their company logo is handy to keep on their desk, in their drawer, or next to them, as a reminder to tell less, and ask more.

 Head over to the MBM shop to pick up a branded deck.

Insight #2: Facebook

Facebook (Meta) is one of the world's most influential social media platforms, and as it was founded with a mission to connect people globally. It's an intriguing paradox that a platform built on people seems to emphasise profit significantly in its annual report.

Throughout our analysis, we found that Facebook's annual report reveals a robust focus on 'profit' related terms. This focus isn't entirely surprising since Facebook is a for-profit entity that is running in an intensely competitive – and ever evolving – digital landscape. Its business model is based on leveraging user data to drive targeted advertising, which is a highly profitable venture, despite its ethical considerations.

People and Profit Focused Trend

Facebook's 2020 annual report showed a very high ratio of **1: 3.1**, with 2021 only making a minor improvement at **1: 3.0**. However, it seems as though Facebook took their own motto's advice and started connecting with the people. Their 2022 annual report shows a ratio of **1: 1.3** - definitely heading in the right direction!

- 2020 – 1: 3.1
- 2021 – 1: 3.0
- 2022 – 1: 1.3

'Employee' mentions go from 52 in 2020, to 56 in 2021 to 234 in 2022 – a five-fold increase. Well done Mark!

In light of the increasing emphasis on employee satisfaction in the context of the 'Great Resignation', the 'people' component appears to require more attention. Given that Facebook's entire value proposition revolves around 'people' - connecting them, understanding them, and catering to them - it's indeed ironic that 'people' related terms aren't more prominently featured in its annual report.

For example, its annual reports saw only 8 mentions of the words 'wellbeing' and 'training' received 2 mentions. On the other hand, 'revenue' was mentioned over 257 times, illustrating a clear focus on the profit aspect of the business.

This doesn't suggest that Facebook is not a 'people-focused' company per se, it does, however, suggest that there is a gap in its portrayal as a people-first company. In light of the scandals Facebook experienced during the 2016 US elections, especially regarding the selling of personal data to for-profit companies, this transition from a focus on profit to a focus on people could indeed improve the company's public standing and reputation.

Did You Know?

Over 87 million Facebook users had their data exposed by Facebook during the 2016 'Cambridge Analytica' scandal.

Insight #3: LVMH Moet Hennessy

When you think of the Moet company, you may imagine yourself sitting in a vineyard in France, sipping on a nice glass of Champagne. In fact, this kind of experience may be associated with a highly expensive activity, as most luxury experiences indeed are.

That being said, there is a paradox in our findings. Our assessment of the company's annual report highlighted that there is a higher-than-average emphasis on 'people' related terms. This finding, particularly within the high-fashion and luxury industry – often perceived as less caring towards its employees, sparks intriguing questions.

LVMH surprisingly shows a ratio of **1: 0.6**, which indicates a strong people focus. This raises the question; why do LVMH, a world leader in luxury accentuate 'people' so prominently? The answer to the question requires us to perform a deeper exploration of the company's core values and organisational culture.

As discussed earlier, culture plays a significant role in employee engagement and hence employee satisfaction. LVMH is known for its robust focus on craftsmanship, quality, and heritage, which are deeply rooted in its workforce's skills, creativity, and dedication.

Therefore, a 'people' focus is a strategic necessity to preserve the high standards that define its luxury offerings, as otherwise, a luxurious product becomes no different from one that is mass produced and geared towards the public.

LVMH's approach to employee engagement goes far beyond simply offering in-house training, as educational institutions also recognise its excellence. In fact, the company has over 24 partner schools worldwide, each dedicated to excellent craftsmanship and luxurious goods, again reinforcing its emphasis on quality handmade production and hence, on people.

Did You Know?

LVMH is the world's leading luxury goods group, and in 2022 they had a recorded revenue of €79.2 billion, with an operating income of €21.1 billion.

So, we'd forgive you for assuming that they would have a more profit-focused annual report!

Interestingly, LVMH's people focus in their annual report could also indicate their internal company culture. LVMH might promote a more humanistic corporate culture, prioritising employee welfare and development alongside profitability. Such a culture would help attract and retain talent and foster a motivated workforce that contributes positively to the company's performance.

It's worth noting that LVMH operates in a market where the brand image and customer perception are paramount. In this case, the 'people' represent employees and the luxury consumers that the company caters to. As a result, LVMH spends significant time, effort, and resources to enhance the consumer experience and maintain high brand appeal. This would naturally result in a high frequency of 'people' mentions in their reports, and so it does.

Insight #4: Roche Holdings

Roche Holdings, the healthcare provider, mentions people words three times more than profit words, with a ratio of **1 : 0.3.** You'd expect this being a healthcare provider, but why then do AstraZeneca have a ratio of **1 : 2.7** if that's the case?

Roche Holdings, the Swiss healthcare company, stands at the top of our people to profit ratio league table. This indicates Roche's well-known people-centric approach. For example, their mission statement highlights this:

'Our commitment to our people, partners, stakeholders and, most importantly, our patients remains as strong as it was on the first day of our journey'.

Their focus on developing talent, nurturing their workforce, and maintaining a conducive work environment appears to manifest strongly in their annual reports. Despite being a for-profit organisation, their narrative emphasises people as their foremost asset. It could also signify their belief in employee welfare as a key driver for long-term profits.

What might explain Roche's heightened emphasis on 'people'? Is this a reflection of cultural disparities between American capitalist culture and Swiss approaches to human capital, or are there other factors at play?

Did You Know?

2023 marks the 6th time that Switzerland has been ranked #1 for best quality of life, according to the 2023 Best Countries Report.

Switzerland, where Roche is headquartered, is renowned for its high standard of living, robust social security system, and strong emphasis on worker rights— cultural and socio-political factors that can bring about a more 'people-focused' approach in business practices. That being said, disparities between countries are just one part of the puzzle. Roche's 'people' focus is also likely a reflection of its strategic approach. The company has consistently emphasised innovation, quality, and patient-centricity, all of which rely heavily on its workforce's skills, motivation, and wellbeing.

Roche's commitment to its workforce is well-documented, fostering a culture that emphasises people, their development, and their wellbeing. The company believes in investing in its people, reflected in their employee-centric programs programs and initiatives. The below image shows one of the core values displayed on Roche's website, showing active translation of people-focus.

Engagement: good for our employees, good for our business

We believe that employees who are engaged are key to delivering the highest standards and the greatest levels of innovation. That's why we care about what makes working at Roche a rewarding experience for our employees. We know that many things matter to our employees: health and well-being, having a leader who behaves in a way that supports our values and leadership commitments, as well as having the support to develop your career, the tools to do your job and being recognized when you do it well. That's why we take the time to ask employees for their opinion and measure their engagement through regular global employee surveys. And that's why we then act on the results – to build an ever better place to work for our people.

Image from Roche's Our Values page.

Additionally, Roche has demonstrated a strong commitment to employee development and corporate responsibility. Its initiatives such as 'Roche Continents,' which supports creative projects that 'explore the parallels between innovation in art and in science' and 'Roche Employee Action and Charity Trust (Re&Act)' underscore the value it places on people and community engagement.

Re&Act has been involved in projects that aim to improve menstrual hygiene in Malawian schools. Re&Act have also taken part in a project that provides holistic care with children in Ethiopia, showing a particular attention to respecting local beliefs and traditions, and supporting access to education in Cambodia.

People and Profit Focused Trend

As well as being people-focused, Roche is also consistent. Their 2020 & 2022 annual reports shows a ratio of 1:0.4 and 1:0.3 respectively, in comparison to 2021's 1:0.3. This indicates that 2021 wasn't just a fluke – people-focused is just who they are!

- 2020 – 1:0.4
- 2021 – 1:0.3
- 2022 – 1:0.3

Insight #5: VISA

Visa is a global leader in digital payments, and as expected from a financial company, they score very low on the 'people' keywords with a ratio of 1 : 3.6. That being said, it again represents an interesting case study, particularly because of its depiction as a people-first company, especially in its marketing. For example, its new approach to the circular economy appears to be especially people-focused:

'Action needs to be taken to inspire individuals to rethink the way they shop and consume, because, as the world's climate changes and the cost of living increases, the way we shop has never mattered more. Given the fundamental role of payments in modern global economies and its history in enabling large-scale socio-economic progress through the digital payments revolution, we believe that the payments industry has the power to enable a positive shift towards more sustainable behaviours'.

Despite this apparent focus on people, Visa only mentions people keywords 94 times, while mentioning profit keywords such as income 183 times and profit keywords as a whole over 339 times. Is it truly focused on the people? Of course, like other players in the banking world, Visa is a for-profit company – but as discussed throughout this report, the two are not mutually exclusive.

The company often positions itself as 'for the people', emphasising the role it plays in enabling economic transactions for individuals, businesses, and economies worldwide. Yet, our analysis showcases a somewhat different narrative, one less focused on 'people' than might have been expected.

In 2020, Visa set out key goals to help them improve their diversity. For example, it aimed to improve its inclusion and diversity efforts by 'increasing the number of individuals from historically underrepresented groups at the vice president level and above in the U.S. by 50%' and 'increasing the number of historically under-represented Visa colleagues in the U.S. by 50% by 2025'.

Visa has also launched various learning initiatives, such as Visa University, Visa Learning Hub, Visa Learning Festivals, Educational Assistance, and Partnerships. Thus, the company is making strides to be more people-centric, but its annual accounts nevertheless paint a different picture. Is this a glance into the company's true colours?

Excuse the interruption....

As discussed above, Equity, Diversity and Inclusion is a topical issue in the current work climate, and one which some companies may find difficult to grasp.

Enter the coaching cards!

We have developed a deck of EDI coaching cards in partnership with the NHS (the UK National Health Service with 1.3 million employees) to help you and your team to improve your awareness and understanding of EDI issues.

available at

Insight #6: ASML Holdings

ASML Holdings, a key player in the semiconductor industry, ranks highly at #4 out of 100 with a ratio of **1 : 0.6**. ASML has a reputation for fostering an inclusive and innovative work culture, which could explain the high 'people' mentions in their annual reports. It seems to suggest that ASML perceives its people as essential to maintaining its cutting-edge technologies and market leadership.

A key aspect of ASML's success lies in its commitment to employees' growth and development. With an industry that evolves at a fast pace, ASML has placed a high priority on fostering a learning environment that keeps its workforce at the forefront of technological advancements. Their learning focus can be seen through their use of the 70-20-10 method, which boasts that '70% of learning will be on the job, 20% through coaching, and 10% through training courses'.

ASML's people-oriented approach goes beyond learning and development, as they also take into account wellbeing and mental health. ASML actively acknowledges the role of employee happiness in the success of the company. They mention 'wellbeing' 15 times throughout their annual report, and this is backed up by the 'four wellbeing pillars' that they advocate on their website.

Much like ASML, Sticky Learning ® is also based on the principal of 70:20:10, which was originated by Charles Jennings, who has written many of the forewords on MBM's whitepapers. We have over 7 brilliant whitepapers to aid you in your learning, take a look at a few below:

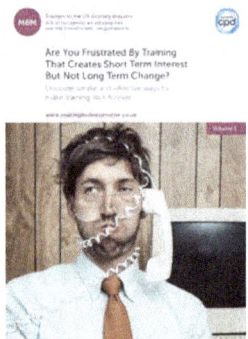  

Insight #7: Royal Dutch Shell

Despite being in the very profit-driven oil and gas industry, Royal Dutch Shell presents a 1 : 0.9 . ratio. This may reflect Shell's recent attempts to portray itself as a socially responsible company. The prominence of 'people' in its annual report may signify efforts to improve employee welfare, customer relationships, and a broader societal impact, possibly as part of its response to environmental concerns and social expectations.

Understanding the context in which Shell operates provides insights into this emphasis. Over recent years, the energy sector has faced mounting social and regulatory pressures to address its environmental impact and contribute to global sustainability goals. This has led to a transformation of the industry, with an increased focus on social responsibility, stakeholder engagement, and employee welfare. Shell's values, which can be seen below, now encompass 'honesty, integrity and respect for the people', which is supported by their 1 : 0.9 ratio.

Furthermore, Shell has faced considerable public scrutiny and has been involved in multiple controversies over its environmental and social impacts. This has likely driven the company to increase its focus on people in its annual reports.

At Shell, we share a set of core values – honesty, integrity and respect for people – which underpin all the work we do. The Shell General Business Principles, Code of Conduct and Ethics and Compliance Manual help everyone at Shell act in line with these values and comply with relevant laws and regulations.

Shell Global
https://www.shell.com › about-us › our-values

Our Values | Shell Global

Image copied from Shell Our Values Page.

By highlighting its commitment to employees, communities, and broader society, Shell seeks to improve its public image and demonstrate its dedication to corporate responsibility.

Topic Analysis

Topic #1: How People Focused is Your Healthcare?

When you think of 'Big Pharma', you most likely think of companies who must care about individuals' wellbeing since, naturally, their products and services are as human-centric as they can get. And yet, this was one of the most significant discoveries made throughout this research: Big Pharma, unfortunately, has some of the absolute lowest ratios of People to Profit keyword mentions.

For example, AstraZeneca plc. had a ratio of **1: 2.7** with 1,116 mentions of Profit words, and 413 people mentions. Whilst Eli Lilly & Co had a ratio of **1: 4.1** with 466 profit mentions and only 1134 people mentions. Surprisingly, AstraZeneca claim in their company values 'We put patients first' however, our data, analysing 'people' focus words doesn't support that.

As such, in 'Big Pharma', the debate around 'people vs profit' takes on a distinctly critical tone. Our analysis of the industry's communications reveals a distinct trend: a higher frequency of 'profit' related words as opposed to 'people' oriented terms. This can be further seen by the graph below, which places each pharmaceutical company in our study (total: 10) against their people versus profit ratio. These findings highlight that 80% of the pharmaceutical companies in this study have a higher profit ratio. Only 2 companies have a ratio of below '1' on profit words; Pfizer and Roche Holdings.

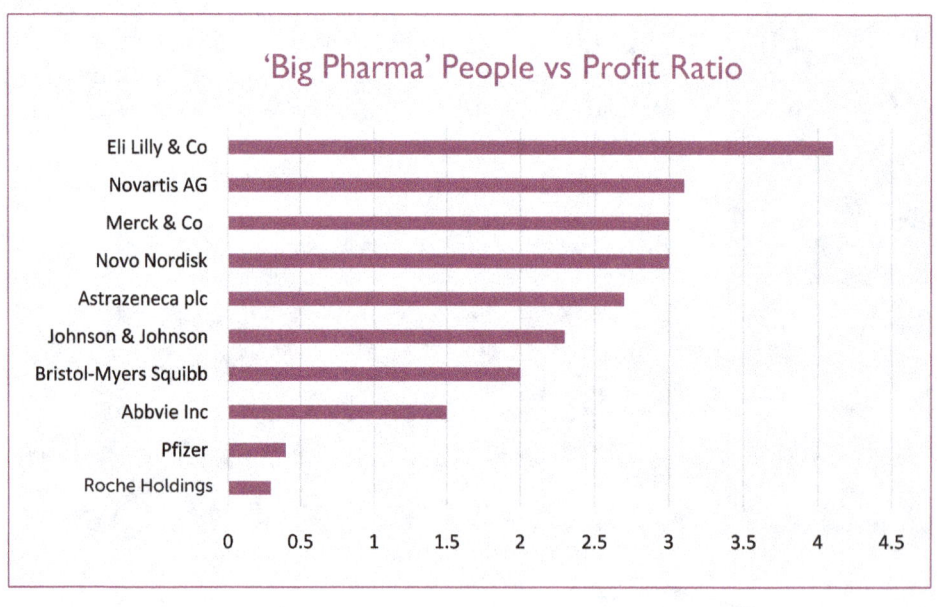

'Big Pharma' People vs Profit Ratio

But what does this imply about Big Pharma's approach, and more importantly, its implications on healthcare? Here, the idea that companies which are profit-focused are not as concerned with people is especially worrying, particularly because of how the very products and services that big pharma offers affect people on a very deep basis (quite literally!).

Indeed, the core function of the pharmaceutical industry is inherently people-focused – developing and producing medications to enhance health and save lives. However, as for-profit entities, pharmaceutical companies are also driven by their economic objectives. After all, they cannot survive without profit. This raises questions surrounding the ethics behind profit-focused companies when they are connected to our health. Still, this debate is beyond the scope of this report.

Please note that this is not to suggest that all pharmaceutical companies or practices are profit-centric or do not place patients' health first – naturally, their annual accounts can only tell us so much, and our conclusions are our own.

For example, there are companies actively investing in employee welfare, patient safety, and social responsibility. That being said, the industry's narrative does seem to lean towards a more profit-driven approach, based on our keyword analysis.

#peoplevsprofit

Topic #2: Are American Banks the Most Money Hungry Banks?

When dissecting the 'people vs profit' focus in different national contexts, an interesting comparison arises between Chinese and American companies, particularly within the banking sector.

> For example, we see that the China Merchants Bank has a People vs Profit ratio of **1: 0.8**, with 983 'people' mentions compared to 784 'profit' mentions. Starkly different from them is Bank of America, with its **1: 2.6** ratio, whereby the report had 299 'people' mentions compared to 784 'profit' mentions.

We can see here that whilst both China Merchants Bank and Bank of America have the same number of profit mentions, when juxtaposed with the number of people mentions, it shows American banks as far more profit-focused.

These differences possibly can in part be traced back to the unique development paths, economic ideologies, and cultural frameworks intrinsic to each nation – the US being especially focused on profit, and the Chinese being more focused on long-term planning.

Specifically, in China, there is a noticeable emphasis on long-term, continual growth, which has been witnessed throughout their many long-term minded approaches to development, such as their investments in African agriculture, among many others. China's focus has largely centred around comprehensive development, which involves a substantial consideration for people, as opposed to focusing more on economic development, a key characteristic of American development. This developmental approach has roots in the country's socialist market economy, where the state plays a dominant role in strategic sectors, such as banking.

Chinese banks often function as extensions of state policy, contributing to national development goals. With this in mind, their 'people' orientation could relate more to society at large, potentially encompassing the wider Chinese population or even the Chinese Communist Party (CCP). However, it's important to clarify that this doesn't imply a lack of attention to profitability. Rather, the focus on people and societal development are seen as means to achieve long-term economic stability and prosperity, and therefore as two elements that aren't mutually exclusive.

On the other hand, American banks operate within a much more capitalist framework that values free-market dynamics and competition, or a system in which the government is minimally or not present at all. In this development pathway, the corporate ethos is largely profit-driven, focusing on aspects like market share, revenue growth, and shareholder returns. **Therefore, it was expected that American banks would be especially profit-focused.**

Cultural nuances also play a crucial role in shaping these differences. For example, in China, there is a certain emphasis on community welfare and collective progress (guided by Confucian values) which tends to align businesses towards a broader societal focus instead of being solely profit-focused. On the other hand, the American ethos, which is completely different and significantly more underpinned by individualism, will drive a more competitive, profit-centric approach, while considering the people who support these efforts as individuals running the capitalist machine.

Finally, the varying GDP per capita levels in the two countries are also something we need to consider. With its higher GDP per capita, the US has a much more mature market. Businesses can focus on maintaining and growing their profit margins, especially since its customers live in a country that is much more accepting of credit usage. On the other hand, China is growing economically and still has a very large population transitioning out of poverty. This means that economic prosperity and inclusive development need to happen, which may inform this focus on people witnessed in banks.

That being said, in recent years, there has indeed been a growing recognition of the role that people – employees, customers, and the wider community – play in driving continued profitability; that is, profitability that remains profitable in future years, as opposed to only be taking place in the short term and promising no long-term longevity. Thus, American banks, are looking to increasingly integrate people-focused strategies, such as employee engagement, customer-centric services, and corporate social responsiblility.

A key example of this increasing awareness of people by American banks is JP Morgan. This company is perhaps the exception that proves the rule of the American and Chinese banks. With a ratio of **1 : 0.7**, JP Morgan emphasises a people-focus in their annual report, contradicting previous notions of America's profit-hungry banks. They also mention 'learning' words a total of 46 times, contributing to a more employee-focused company, with a developmental ideal.

Topic #3: How Seriously are Companies Taking Wellbeing?

Wellbeing in the Face of the Post-Pandemic World

In the wake of the global pandemic, a spotlight has been cast upon the world of work and the practices companies have in place to support employee wellbeing. The graph below shows an upwards trend in use of the word 'wellbeing' in the last five years. Work-life balance, mental health considerations, and an overall emphasis on wellbeing are not just buzzwords but significant factors that define the workplace's ethos today.

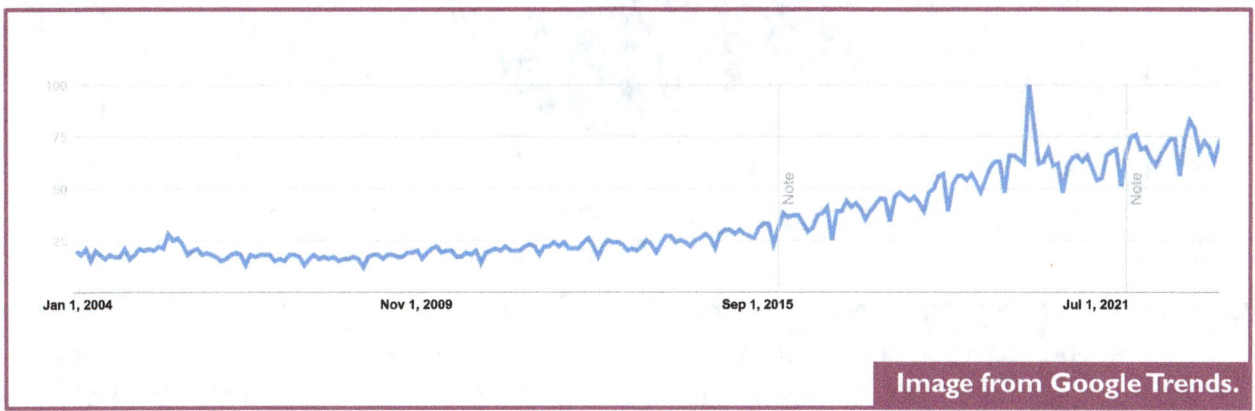

Image from Google Trends.

We can see in the above graph that 'wellbeing' has been rising in interest gradually in the last two decades, with a significant peak during the Covid-19 lockdown of 2020. The prevalence of this topic is why we considered the number of times that the word 'wellbeing' is used in an annual report.

While evaluating the volume of the keyword 'wellbeing', we can see a revealing angle on its perceived importance. That being said, we also need to acknowledge that 'true' corporate commitment to employee wellbeing extends far beyond its lexical presence in public communications – it is found in initiatives, projects and ways of working.

"This report brings to life the increasingly prevalent conversations I am having with business leaders the world over. Those conversations focus on the difficulties that organisations are facing when trying to choose between people or profit in an increasingly CA world". - **Bobbi Hartshorne, Founder and Chief Wellbeing Officer (CWO), WellWise**.

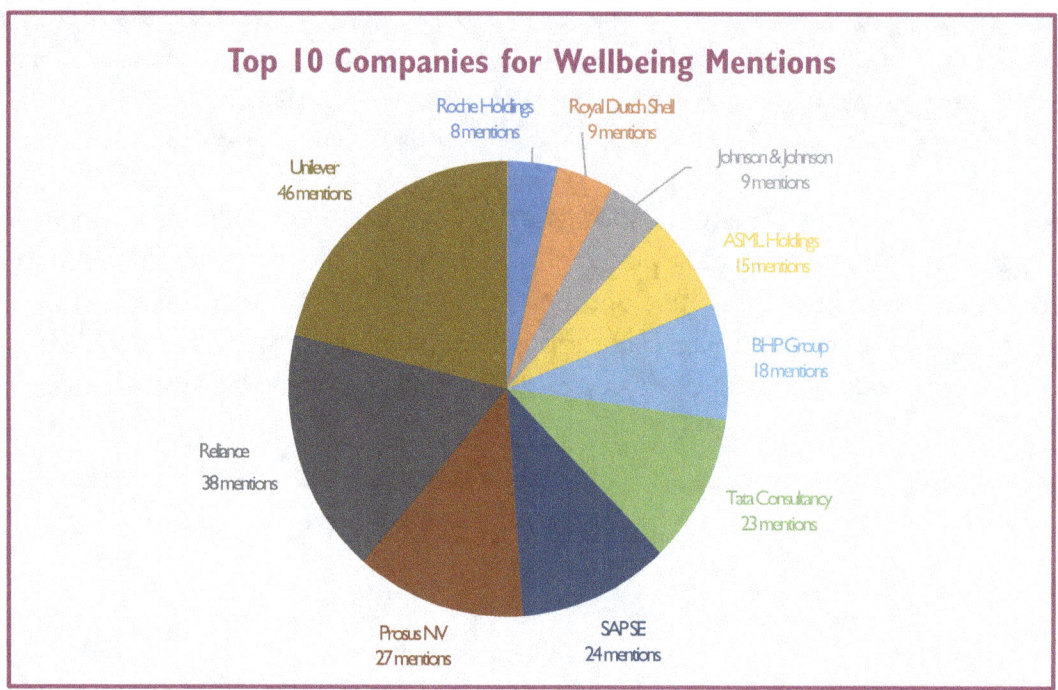

Top 10 Companies for Wellbeing Mentions

Our analysis of corporate annual reports shows that the attention companies give to 'wellbeing' varies widely. Unilever leads the pack with 46 mentions of 'wellbeing', perhaps unsurprisingly, given the company's focus on humanity. However, close on their heels, is Reliance Industries with 38 mentions and Prosus with 27 mentions. It's interesting to observe companies from diverse industries - from software to semiconductors - highlighting the importance of wellbeing, indicating a broad trend across sectors.

Another interesting insight is from SAP SE, who have 24 mentions of 'wellbeing' in their annual report. This could be seen as somewhat surprising given the company's relative youth, founded in 1972. However, perhaps the influence of its five founders, who pioneered a new era of software development, still permeates the company's culture. Their forward-thinking approach may well extend to employee wellbeing, reflecting a more modern understanding of work culture that values employee health and happiness as key contributors to productivity and innovation.

Expectedly, Johnson and Johnson, a company rooted in healthcare, makes the list with 9 mentions. However, it's striking to see it outranked by younger tech firms, raising questions about the evolving values and priorities within different industries and generations of companies.

Also noteworthy is Tata Consultancy making a significant appearance with 23 'wellbeing' mentions. This reaffirms the increasing importance of employee wellbeing in the IT and consulting sector, known for its challenging work environment.

Did You Know?

An alarming 34% of the companies in our 100-company sample do not mention 'wellbeing' even once in their annual reports. That's a third of companies that are probably not addressing the trending topic of wellbeing at all in their reports, and possibly not in their company culture.

This glaring omission raises critical questions. Is it due to a lack of focus on employee wellbeing, or are these companies simply not communicating their efforts? In today's competitive talent market, where potential employees have a growing awareness and demand for workplaces that support their wellbeing, such an omission could impact these companies' attractiveness as employers. While these are indeed annual accounts, one may expect that employee wellbeing would at least be mentioned once, particularly considering the greater emphasis placed on employees' mental and physical health due to Covid-19, and the consequential ramifications.

What About Mental Health?

We cannot talk about wellbeing without mentioning mental health too. The two go hand in hand and are both something that companies should be taking into consideration and then reflecting in their annual reports. Alongside searching the annual reports for 'wellbeing' and 'wellness' mentions, we also searched the reports for 'mental health' mentions. To give a broad overview, we added these three together to achieve a total which we've coined 'care words'.

Company	Total Care Mentions	Care Ranking
Reliance INDS	59	#1
Unilever plc	59	#2
PayPal Holdings	49	#3
Prosus NV	44	#4
BHP Group Ltd	42	#5
Tata Consultancy	41	#6
SAP SE	32	#7
AIA	27	#8
Bank of America	26	#9
ASML Holding NV	21	#10

Insight #1: The Key is in the Specifics

While reviewing these figures, it was interesting to see that a number of these top 5 wellbeing focused companies have specific programs and initiatives for their team members, and some even have access for their family members too.

A key example of this is Reliance Industries and their 21-day program focusing on the International Day of Happiness. Different events were arranged throughout their organisation with a major focus on mental health. Another example, SAP SE sponsored a Mental Health Day on April 27th, 2021, throughout their company with a similar focus.

Therefore, employee wellbeing includes much more than free lunches or the ability to work from home. It involves all kinds of elements: physical and mental health, social connections, opportunities for growth & development, and many more, all depending on what the company offers and how it offers it. It's part of an environment that not only values its people for their professional contributions but also supports their development and welfare as a whole person.

Insight #2: How 'Caring' are the Top 100 Companies?

Something quite shocking that we discovered when compiling this 'care' category, was that 21 companies do not mention any 'care' words (wellbeing, wellness or mental health throughout their entire 2021 annual report. Now, this is particularly concerning because 2021 was the period in which we had just emerged from the pandemic, and mental health had really suffered. Additionally, 3 of those 21 companies that didn't mention care words include Apple, Google and Costco – big names which you would expect to address such a topical issue, but they don't address it at all in their annual report. Even Donald Trump addresses this crucial issue in his December 2019 speech!

Insight #3: Big Cheer for BHP

We feel it only right to share the company that mentioned mental health the most in their 2021 annual report, and that was BHP with a whopping 23 mentions. Their focus on mental health within their annual report can perhaps be attributed to their involvement treatments in for mental health conditions, or various campaigns that are involved in like Mental Health Month 2023.

Excuse the interruption....

The need to understand mental health is more crucial than ever, as is understanding the correct tools to aid people's mental health.

We've written a Mental Health Toolkit, with 35 different tools for you to utilise to enable you to become the best version of yourself.

Share this with your staff to help them achieve their best mental health and increase the happiness of your team.

Mental Health Toolkit of 35 Tools to Achieve Your Best Mental Health

The Need for a Mental Health Toolkit is Never More Needed Than Now

The Google Trends graph below shows the popularity of people searching for 'mental health' in the last decade. Consequently, this Mental Health Toolkit will help to satisfy this growing interest.

A company that sees its people primarily as 'employees' might be viewing its workforce through a narrower lens (i.e. as someone who only matters within the company four walls), which might be limiting its approach to staff wellbeing.

To bring this research to the current day, it's important to note the 'back to work' initiative that many companies are implementing. A staggering 90% of companies plan to have people back in the office by the end of 2024. And, even more astonishing than this number, is the 30% of companies that said they would threaten to fire employees who don't comply with in-office requirements.

This news really supports the low number of companies that mention wellbeing and mental health in their annual reports, because to force employees to be in the office five days a week rebuffs any ideas of flexibility, wellness, and productivity.

Whilst it's been suggested that productivity is lower when working from home, the idea of going zero to one hundred, by asking people to commute in five days a week again, could leave many employees with financial and emotional troubles. Those with anxiety, or a range of other mental health issues may serve a company much better with at least some days working from home, but it appears that for 90%, this idea has been disregarded.

Did You Know?

Goldman Sachs wants employees in five days a week, and Google will be factoring employees' in-office attendance into their performance reviews.

BE THE BEST VERSION OF YOURSELF

EXPERT INTERVIEWS

MBM PODCASTS

If you'd like to hear more about mental health, and why we should all be talking about it, take a listen to our Expert Interview podcast with Simon Blake, CEO of Mental Health England.

MHFA England

This is just one of hundreds of podcasts on our website. Head over to 'Making Business Matter Podcasts' to find out more.

Wellbeing Over the Years

As aforementioned, the top 3 companies for 'wellbeing' mentions are Unilever, Reliance Industries and Prosus. To compare with these top 3, we've chosen 3 companies that did not mention 'wellbeing' at all: Amazon, Intel, and China Mobile. We have looked at these 6 companies 2020 and 2022 annual reports also to see if this high, and low, focus on 'wellbeing' is a fluke, or who they are.

Exactly as we searched for 'wellbeing' in the 2021 annual reports, we did the same with the 2020 and 2022 reports, to get a better overview of the three companies' 'wellbeing' focus, or perhaps lack of. Below is the resulting table that allows us to see 'wellbeing' mentions for each of these 6 companies, across 3 years.

Company	2020	2021	2022
Unilever	39	46	92
Reliance Industries	22	38	44
Prosus	31	27	12
Amazon	0	0	0
Intel	0	0	1
China Mobile	0	0	0

So, what can we take from viewing these companies over 3 years rather than just 12 months? Well, the first glaring insight is that from the small 3-company sample of Amazon, Intel, and China Mobile, we can see that companies that didn't mention 'wellbeing' in their 2021 annual reports likely haven't been mentioning them at all, over the years. Both Amazon and China Mobile, haven't mentioned 'wellbeing' once in the last 3 years in their annual reports.

The lack of wellbeing mentions could attest to the values that the company hold dear and does not show these companies favourably.

We could perhaps expect this from Amazon as they recently outpaced Walmart as 'the nation's fiercest anti-union employer'. It has come to light that the average Amazon warehouse worker only lasts eight months before leaving, and this has been put down to the lack of 'people-focus', suggesting that the Amazon giant simply treats people as robots. A sentiment that is wholly supported by their annual reports.

In contrast, we can see those companies that were in the top 3 for 'wellbeing' mentions, have remained on the podium with a high number of mentions across all 3 of their reports. Unilever had a steady increase of mentions from 2020 to 2021 before landing a whopping 92 mentions in their most recent 2022 report.

Similarly, Reliance Industries has been steadily increasing their focus on 'wellbeing', doubling their number of mentions from 22 mentions in 2020 to 44 mentions in 2022. For both Unilever and Reliance, this suggests that putting the emphasis on wellbeing is simply who these companies are, rather than a front they are putting on for the 2021 report.

An anomaly that we can see in our table is Prosus. It seems that unlike Unilever and Reliance, Prosus has headed the other way, steadily decreasing the number of mentions from 31 in 2020 to just 12 in their 2022 report.

There could be several reasons for this change; a conscious effort to focus more on their profits this year, a change in leadership, or simply that they mentioned other 'people' words more instead of 'wellbeing'. Although they have seen a decrease in mentions, 12 in their 2022 report still outshines many companies with less than 10 or even zero mentions across all three years (ahem – Amazon). To give a broader picture, across all 100 companies, the average 'wellbeing' mentions was 4 mentions. In an average word count of 99,145 words, this is a mention every 50 pages of a 200 page report.

Wellness vs Wellbeing

In order to get a fully rounded picture of how companies view wellbeing, we decided to also count the number of times that the word 'wellness' was mentioned. For two reasons, to see if there is a correlation between 'wellness' and 'wellbeing', and also in case companies used 'wellness' instead of 'wellbeing' and therefore we were being too harsh. So to start, the table below shows the top 5 companies in terms of 'wellness' mentions, alongside the number of times they mentioned 'wellbeing'.

Company	Wellbeing Mentions	Wellness Mentions
PayPal	38	4
AIA	20	6
Bank of America	19	3
Philip Morris	13	2
Prosus NV	10	27

The first takeaway from the table above is that compared to the 33 companies that didn't mention 'wellbeing', there were 57 companies that didn't mention 'wellness', which perhaps suggests that it is a less commonly used term.

Secondly, it's interesting to note that Phillip Morris is #4 for number of 'wellness' mentions yet ranks #81 for people to profit ratio (**1: 3.5**). This indicates that whilst they put a high focus on 'wellness', that might be the only part of people that they do put a focus on.

Our table below shows the top 10 companies for 'wellness' and 'wellbeing' when added together. Interestingly, Paypal comes in at #3 when both of the mentions are added together, but Roche are no longer in the top 10 as they don't mention 'wellness' at all.

Surprisingly, both Bank of America and Philip Morris have high people to profit ratios, meaning that they mention 'profit' words considerably more than 'people' words. However, they score highly on 'wellness' and 'wellbeing' mentions, which you would expect more from companies with a stronger focus on people.

Company	Total Mentions for Wellness & Wellbeing	People vs Profit Ratio
Unilever	49	1 : 1.4
Reliance	44	1 : 1.3
PayPal	42	1 : 0.8
Prosus	39	1 : 1.1
Tata Consultancy	31	1 : 1.2
AIA	26	1 : 1.6
Bank of America	22	1 : 2.6
BHP Group	19	1 : 1.6
AMSL Holdings	15	1 : 0.6
Philip Morris	15	1 : 3.5

It appears that a high number of 'wellbeing' mentions doesn't necessarily equal a high number of 'wellness' mentions. If we look at Unilever and Reliance who are in the top 3 for 'wellbeing' mentions, they don't have a particularly high number of 'wellness' mentions, which would suggest that perhaps it's simply a case of each company using different terms rather than using 'wellbeing' and 'wellness' interchangeably.

However, the top 5 companies for 'wellness' mentions all have 'wellbeing' mentions of more than 2. This indicates that if a company doesn't mention 'wellbeing' it probably doesn't mention 'wellness'.

Following on from this, a total of 28 companies don't mention either 'wellbeing' or 'wellness' throughout the entirety of their annual report. Now, we don't like to name and shame... or do we? Take a look at the 28 culprits below:

- Abbot Labs
- Agricultural Bank of China
- Alibaba
- Alphabet
- Apple
- AT&T
- Boeing
- Bristol-Myer
- Broadcomm
- Charter Communications
- Chevron
- China Mobile
- Costco

- Kweichow Moutai
- Nextera Energy
- Novartis AG
- Ping AN
- Sony Group
- Tesla Inc
- Texas Instrument
- Toyota
- Verizon Communications
- VISA
- Volkswagen AG
- The Walt Disney Company
- Wells Fargo & Co

- Siemens
- China Construction Bank

> The most astonishing companies on this list are The Walt Disney Company, Google (Alphabet) and Apple, as three of the biggest household names.

Excuse the interruption....

As we just have spent quite a few pages saying, wellbeing is important. Especially in the increasingly isolated world that we live, and work, in. It's both the job of your company and the job of you to look after your own wellbeing.

To help you that task, we have a few helpful blog posts discussing various elements of wellbeing. Here are a few of our favourites:

- Employee Empowerment & Wellbeing
- Resilience & Wellbeing Today: The Big Bounce Back
- Reflection: The Importance of Emotional Wellbeing

Our blog has over 1,000 posts (we're very proud of it), and wellbeing is one of hundreds of topics we cover in order to help you become the best version of yourself.

Topic #4: Are These Giants Green?

Recently, Prince William announced the prize winners for the Royal Foundation's third Earthshot Award, which got us thinking about an added element to our report. How green are the big companies? Much like wellbeing, environmental awareness and sustainability are topics that have become hotspots in recent years, with many companies creating sustainability campaigns and projects to remain relevant and ethical.

So, we added a 'green words' section to our research and searched the 2021 annual reports for the words 'environmental' and 'sustainability' to see how much of a focus the top 100 companies put on our planet.

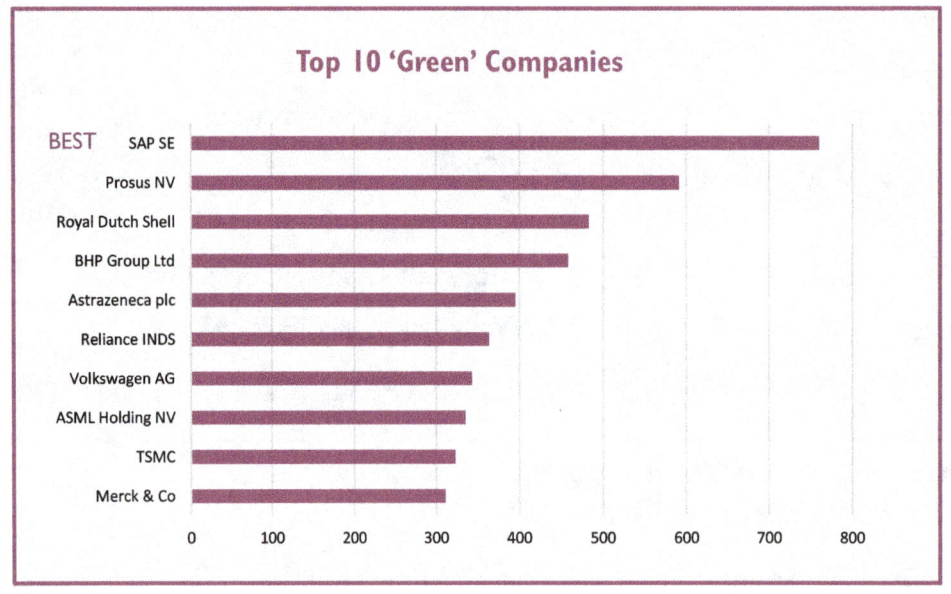

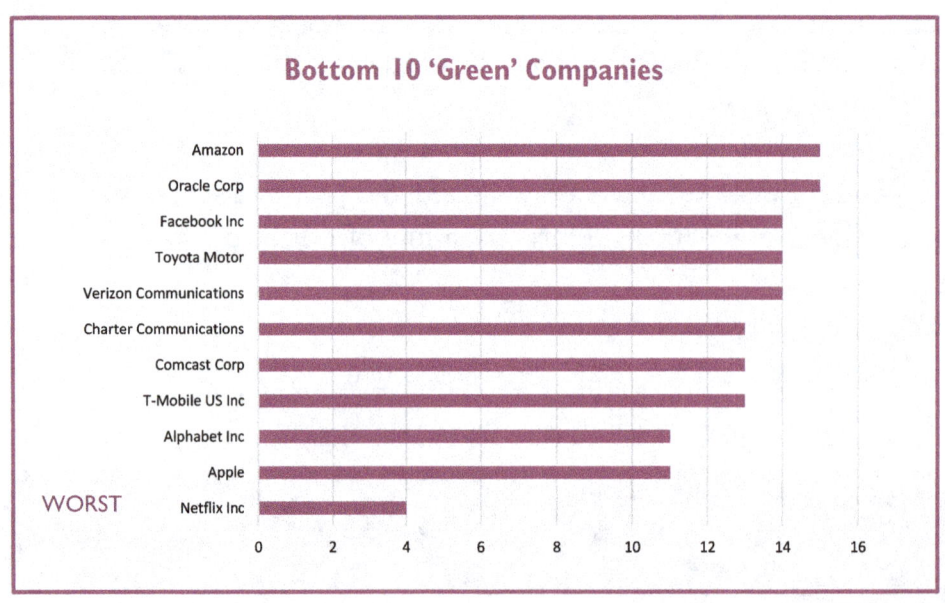

Insight #1: Too Big to Be Green?

One of the most shocking insights from our 'green' research is that the bottom 3 companies in 'green' mentions are some of the biggest household names: Netflix, Apple, and Google (Alphabet). Now, whilst we must consider that the nature of their industries would suggest a lower number of green mentions than say, energy companies, for the top 100 companies, we would still expect a higher level of environmental awareness. A level of awareness that is communicated through their annual report, because they have a responsibility to everyone to lead by example. It seems as though both Apple and Google are focusing more on the 'green' as the years go on, because their 2022 reports increase in 'green' mentions, from 11 to 18 and 11 to 44 respectively. However, Netflix remained stagnant with the exact same number of green mentions in both their 2021 and 2022 reports.

Insight #2: A Surprising Show from Shell

The next thing to point out is the fact that the high ranking of Shell is perhaps to be expected, considering their standing as a 'big oil'. They rank #3 for 'green' mentions which you may hope for as they should be environmentally conscious given the nature of the industry. However, Shell's recent 'green' advert was banned in the UK for 'being likely to mislead'. The advert was accused of not telling viewers that most of their business is based on fossil fuels which are, environmentally speaking, very harmful. This disparity between Shell's annual report and their messaging perhaps suggests a need to better mirror their report.

Insight #3: How Do They Compare?

Our final insight looks at a comparison between what the annual reports are saying and Sustainability Magazine's Top 100 Companies. Interestingly, Sustainability Mag lists Amazon as #11 for most sustainable companies which contrasts their 'green' ranking in our league table of #90. This could demonstrate a disconnect between the reality of their achievements in sustainability versus our question of; in 44,967 words, why do they only use 15 'green' words, which is 0.0003%?

It seems that this is still a problem for Amazon because 'green' mentions in their more recent 2022 annual report shows a total of 14. So rather than increasing their environmental focus, it appears they are going backwards instead, according to their annual report.

"The exploration of sustainability uncovers startling insights, emphasizing a concerning lack of focus from major global companies." **- Steve Lister, Sustainability Consultant**

Topic #5: Do Equality, Diversity, and Inclusion Make the Cut?

Much like the 'green' words, we felt it only right to take a peek into the very topical world of EDI. We searched the 2021 annual reports for three words; 'equality', 'diversity' and 'inclusion' and wanted to share a few insights with you. Below we have shared the top and bottom 10 companies for 'EDI' mentions.

Company	EDI Mentions	Ranking
Prosus NV	140	#1
Nike Inc	115	#2
Bank of America	111	#3
ASML Holding NV	102	#4
Unilever plc	99	#5
Royal Dutch Shell	98	#6
BHP Group Ltd	90	#7
Astrazeneca plc	88	#8
United Parcel	88	#9
Paypal Holdings	85	#10
Industrial & Commercial Bank of China	2	#91
Oracle Corp	2	#92
Samsung Electronics	2	#93
Union Pac Corp	2	#94
Broadcom Inc	1	#95
China Construction Bank	1	#96
Nextera Energy	1	#97
Kweichow Moutai	0	#98
Toyota Motor	0	#99
Wuliangye Yibin	0	#100

Insight #1: A Serious Lack of EDI

Perhaps the most interesting insight is that three companies mentioned no 'EDI words' at all in their EDI reports: Wuliangye Yibin, Toyota, and Kweichow Moutai. Failing to mention any of these three very key words surrounding people doesn't show these three companies particularly favourably. In Toyota's case, their lack of 'EDI words' in their annual report is very contrasting to their ethos projected online. On their website they highlight their 'employee networks' which include a LGBTQ+ network and a diverse abilities network. The image below is taken from their website and shows a key focus on EDI.

Image from Toyota's Diversity, Equity, and Inclusion Page.

Our thinking is, maybe, websites are led by marketing whereas annual reports are led by the leaders. Hence the disparity, maybe?

Insight #2: The Younger the Company the Better the EDI?

Another point of interest is that the number of 'EDI words' seems to have no correlation to the age of the company. You may assume that the younger, more modern, companies would have a more significant focus on equality, diversity and inclusion as their values may include more modern ideals like these. However, the most modern company, Alphabet, (founded in 2015) ranks #89 for EDI, with zero mentions of 'equality' or 'diversity' and only 2 mentions of the word 'inclusion', across their 31,808-word annual report. In contrast, the oldest company, Procter & Gamble (founded in 1837) ranks in the top quarter at #25. They have a total of 36 'EDI' mentions, suggesting that perhaps the more modern companies need to highlight a stronger focus on EDI.

Insight #3: Excel in EDI, Excel Overall?

Finally, it's important to note that the companies ranking highly for 'EDI' mentions are not necessarily ranking highly in the overall people to profit ratio. For example, our #2, Nike, and #3, Bank of America, for 'EDI' mentions rank #61 (**1: 2.3**) and #67 (**1: 2.6**), respectively, for people to profit ratio overall. This suggests that whilst a focus on EDI is important in today's working world, these companies may need to look at having a more rounded approach to their people focus.

* Disclaimer: when searching the report for our 'EDI words' we used 'equality' not 'equity'. It's important to note that some companies may have used 'equity' in reference to EDI topics. However, we felt it confusing to search for 'equity' as a term in the annual reports as this also brings up financial topics.

Global Comparisons

Comparison #1: Battle of the Tech Giants: Sony vs Microsoft vs Apple vs Samsung

	Sony	Microsoft	Apple	Samsung
People word mentions	265	276	121	168
Profit word mentions	188	480	281	1,187
People vs Profit ratios	1: 0.7	1: 1.7	1: 2.3	1: 7.1

Our examination of annual accounts from Sony, Microsoft, Apple and Samsung reveals varying priorities and narratives of these leading technology companies. Regarding the 'people vs profit' discussion, our quantitative analysis uncovered intriguing disparities in the emphasis placed on 'people' and 'profit' keywords.

For Samsung, with 168 'people' mentions and 1,187 'profit' mentions, the resulting ratio stands at 1: 7.1. This striking 'people to profit' ratio suggests that Samsung's strategic narrative leans heavily towards profit-related aspects. Despite its global reputation for innovation, this data could be interpreted as Samsung underemphasising the role and value of its people – its workforce and customers – in its communications.

This is not to suggest Samsung disregards its people. Still, perhaps their narrative could be more balanced to align with the growing expectations of socially responsible and people centric corporate behaviours. A balanced people to profit ratio is especially important in light of their statement that 'a company is its people', as we can see below. It appears as though Samsung's statement is not in line with its annual report.

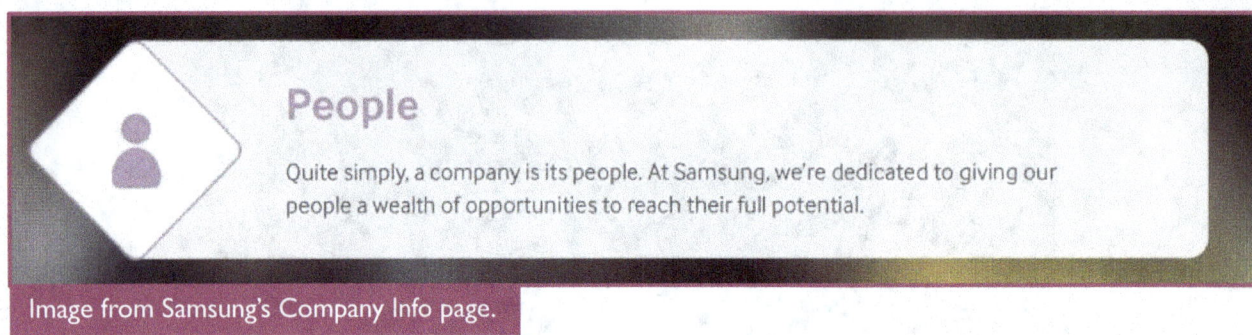

People

Quite simply, a company is its people. At Samsung, we're dedicated to giving our people a wealth of opportunities to reach their full potential.

Image from Samsung's Company Info page.

On the other hand, Apple's communication analysis reveals a slightly different picture. With 121 'people' mentions and 281 'profit' mentions, Apple's 'people to profit' ratio sits at **1: 2.3**, meaning they mention 'profit' words over twice as many times as 'people' words. The ratio suggests a more balanced approach in Apple's annual report, certainly in comparison to Samsung. This is perhaps because it is reflecting its customer-centric philosophy and reputation for prioritising user experience in its product designs.

Harvard Business Review mentioned that Apple is organised for innovation. The article commented that 'Apple's leaders believe that world-class talent wants to work for, and with, other world-class talent in a specialty. It's like joining a sports team where you get to learn from, and play, with the best'. This article from Harvard Business Review suggests that Apple has a more people-focused approach than Samsung. Yet, the absence of 'wellbeing' in its annual 46,576-word annual report may suggest a different reality, potentially obscuring its efforts in this area.

Apple's efforts to introduce more people-oriented actions can be seen by their introduction of new training to support IT members in 2022. However, this is perhaps of little compensation after the 2021 #AppleToo movement which shook the company. The movement related to alleged harassment and discrimination in the organisation.

The issue was addressed by their CEO, Tim Cook, in November 2021 sharing a message supporting the employees' rights to speak about issues within the company. This can perhaps explain why their profit-focus is less than some of its technology competitors. Hopefully, their 'people vs profit' figures continue to improve to support this narrative.

Image courtesy of The Times of India.

Sony starkly contrasts Samsung and Apple, with 265 'people' mentions and only 188 'profit' mentions, resulting in a 'people to profit' ratio of **1: 0.7**. Sony's ratio indicates a strong 'people' focus in their annual report and suggests that Sony prioritises the role of people – both its workforce and customers. This could reflect Sony's long-standing commitment to fostering creativity and inspiring its employees and customers through innovative, high-quality products. In fact, the company states the following on their website:

'As with the business, our basic approach to the people strategy since Sony's foundation has been that each of our diverse employees should be independent and influence each other. This way the value created by our 110,000 diverse employees worldwide is maximised. Around the axis of Individuals, we define the HR Strategy based on People Philosophy as Attract, Develop and Engage Talented Individuals'.

Microsoft stands somewhere between Samsung and Sony. They are only slightly more people-focused than Apple, with 276 'people' mentions and 480 'profit' mentions, which gives them a resulting 'people to profit' ratio of **1: 1.7**. This lower ratio highlights a creep towards becoming more people-focused.

Following years of ongoing criticism and allegations of harassment, sexual discrimination, and misconduct towards junior staff, Microsoft needed to change their focus. In 2020, the company published a statement that they were taking a people-first approach, which can perhaps account for their lower ratio than other technology companies that we have discussed.

However, in comparison to Sony, for example, Microsoft is still showing an emphasis on profit, according to its annual report. This suggests that their communications may not fully reflect their investments in people-centric initiatives such as employee welfare, diversity and inclusion, and customer service. Is it perhaps 'too little, too late' following the years of criticism?

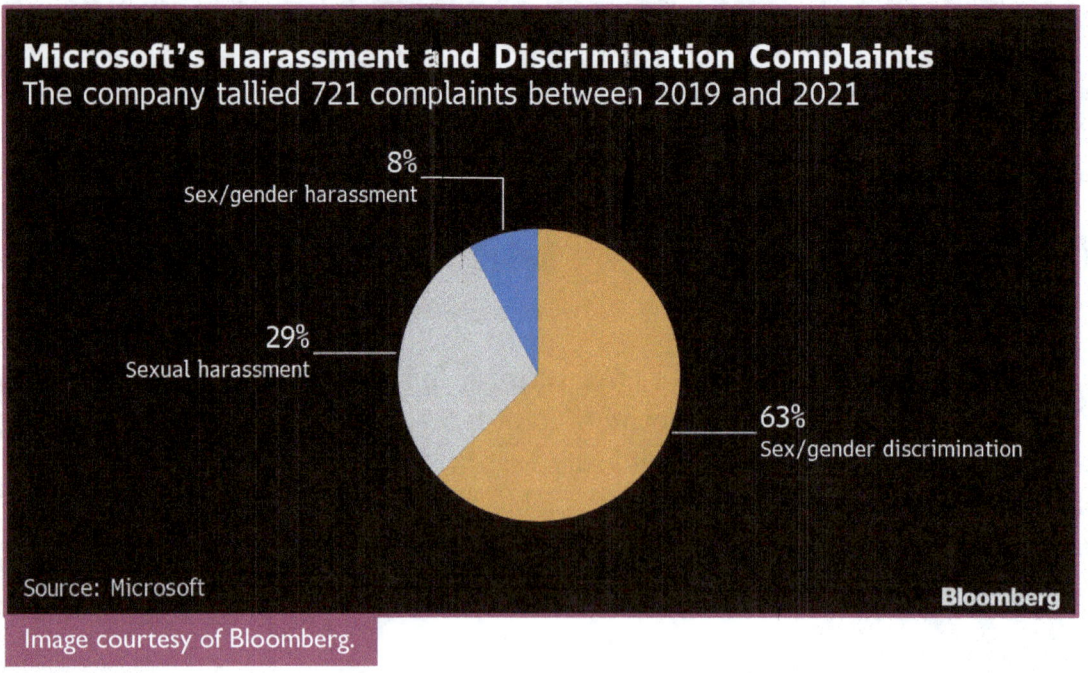

Image courtesy of Bloomberg.

As the world moves towards greater corporate transparency and social responsibility, an imbalance between 'people' and 'profit' in corporate narrative may not bode well. Public narratives that favour profits over people might result in reputational risks in an era where stakeholders increasingly value people-centric approaches. Microsoft is taking strides to address this; and perhaps the 2023 report will show further improvements, gearing towards a focus on the people.

Did You Know?

Microsoft ranks 3rd on Fortune's 'Most Admired Companies' list despite the scrutiny that they have been under for alleged corruption and bribes as well as employee neglect and misconduct.

Microsoft's mid-position of #48 in our league table of people to profit ratio (1: 1.7) is in contrast to Fortune's podium placement of #3.

Perhaps their annual report is not mirroring their company culture?

The findings of this report offer a snapshot into the annual accounts of Sony, Microsoft, Apple, and Samsung. The different 'people to profit' ratios could underscore these companies' varying emphasis on their people versus their profits. This data should not be interpreted as a reflection of these companies' actual practices but rather as a depiction of the priorities expressed in their annual reports.

A company's narrative plays a crucial role in shaping its image and reputation, and the right balance between people and profit can influence stakeholder perception, customer loyalty, and employee satisfaction. Perhaps, moving forward, both Microsoft, Apple and Samsung can consider some of the practices that Sony has in place, at least in terms of their communication references to people and profit.

#peoplevsprofit

Comparison #2: Drink Duel: Coca-Cola vs Pepsi

	Coca-Cola	Pepsi
People word mentions	185	205
Profit word mentions	90	430
People vs Profit ratios	1 : 0.5	1 : 2.1

When we evaluate the 'people vs profit' narratives within Pepsi and Coca-Cola, we uncover compelling insights that could reflect the companies' distinctive strategic orientations. While competing in the same market, these two beverage industry titans appear to prioritise 'people' and 'profit' differently in their annual reports.

For Coca-Cola, with 'people' mentions standing at 185 and 'profit' mentions at 90, the resulting 'people to profit' ratio is 1 : 0.5. This ratio implies that Coca-Cola maintains a more balanced narrative between people and profit. While it recognises the importance of profitability for the longevity of the business, it also seems to place significant emphasis on people – a category that includes not only its workforce but also its consumers and wider communities.

Coca-Cola's #3 ranking in our people to profit ratio league table could reflect their commitment to societal engagement, as demonstrated by its various corporate social responsibility initiatives, like their 'World Without Waste' campaign, launched in 2018. Coca-Cola very clearly outlines principles on its website, as well as their efforts for its sustainability which aligns with their people-focused annual report. Alongside this, they have diversity programmes and community development projects, which all support their high ranking in our people to profit league table.

In contrast, whilst Coca-Cola is using 'profit' words half as many times as 'people' words, Pepsi do the opposite. With 205 'people' mentions and 430 'profit' mentions, Pepsi's ratio indicates a considerably more profit-oriented narrative. Certain scandals like their 2017 advertisement, which trivialised police brutality in the United States, suggests that their profit focused annual report aligns with the messages that they are sending out in other areas.

In a world where corporate responsibility, stakeholder engagement, and people-centric approaches are becoming increasingly more important, these ratios offer a lens to assess how these companies are aligning their narratives with these evolving expectations. While profitability is undoubtedly a critical element for corporate durability, a perceived overemphasis on profit at the expense of people can potentially invite reputational risks.

Did You Know?

Coca-Cola has been the market leader in soft drinks since 2004 with Pepsi ranking second for almost two decades.

Seems as though Pepsi need to fizz up their people words if they want that #1 spot.

These insights from Coca-Cola and Pepsi, underscore the differences that can occur even within the same industry, and between companies that have been competing so closely for years. Pepsi's data particularly suggests that perhaps a high emphasis on people in their annual report may give them the edge on Coca-Cola that they desire.

Comparison #3: Connectivity Comparison: Facebook vs Google

	Facebook	Google
People word mentions	165	62
Profit word mentions	488	270
People vs Profit ratios	1: 3.0	1: 4.4

In the tech industry, the titans of our digital age, Facebook, and Alphabet (Google's parent company), have distinctly different narratives regarding people and profit. A closer look at the numbers reveals stark differences between these two tech behemoths.

With 165 'people' mentions and 488 'profit' mentions, Facebook has a 'people to profit' ratio of **1: 3.0**, meaning they mention profit words three times more than people words. Whilst Facebook's key motto and ethos is around connecting people, their heavy skew towards profit contradicts this. This ratio is perhaps why various they have faced controversies over the years, such as privacy concerns, data misuse and its role in political manipulation.

These controversies may have created a disconnect between Facebook's 'people' narrative and the public perception of its actions. Though Facebook have stated a mission of 'bringing the world closer together', it seems they have perhaps forgotten to put this into practice themselves in their annual report.

Similarly, Alphabet's 'people to profit' ratio sits at **1: 4 .4** with 62 'people' mentions versus 270 'profit' mentions. This slanted ratio is perhaps surprising given Google's widely known motto '[Don't be evil,](#)' which was seen as a commitment to ethical conduct. While Google has taken significant steps to improve user experience and [employee welfare,](#) it hasn't been immune to [scandals and controversies.](#) The company has faced criticisms over antitrust issues, data privacy, and employee relations. A higher emphasis on 'profit' in its communications might reinforce public perceptions that Alphabet is straying from its original people-focused ethos towards a more profit-driven approach.

Image courtesy of Adidio Digital.

The digital age is driven by data and connectivity, where companies like Facebook and Alphabet hold immense power over societal discourse and individual lives. In such a scenario, these 'people vs profit' ratios are more than just numbers; they could provide insight into the narratives these companies promote. The emphasis on 'profit' over 'people' could raise questions about their commitment to their users' welfare, the very people who contribute to their profit. This serves as a reminder that while corporations should be profitable, they must also uphold their responsibilities towards their employees, users, and the wider society.

The disconnect between Facebook's and Google's annual reports and their perceived actions, can potentially undermine their reputation and trust with stakeholders. It is an indicator that, moving forward, these tech giants may need to address the balance between 'people' and 'profit' in their annual reports to maintain their credibility in an increasingly socially conscious world.

Did You Know?

Google may all be fun and games at their HQ but their **1: 4.4** ratio puts them at #92 out of 100 companies in terms of people to profit ratio

How can they make their company more people focused? If only there was somewhere to look that up...

The disparity between Facebook's and Google's mottos and their ratios showcases that their ethos may mainly be something that they discuss on the outside, without truly putting in the work to make this a reality. When we think of companies such as Google, we normally imagine a workplace with free food, pods to nap in, and other similar amenities. Indeed, we've all seen the videos of the snack cupboards and slides! And yet, the fact that their profit mentions are 4 times higher than their people mentions may suggest that this may only be a front.

Something interesting to note is the fact that Google have recently been 'cutting hundreds of jobs globally', which suggests that although their annual report is particularly profit-focused, their profits are perhaps not where they should be, hence the decision to layoff 6% of its global workforce. It begs the question that, maybe if they put more of an emphasis on the people, this may reflect in a more productive workforce that generates the profits they seem to need.

Comparison #4: Superstore Sweep: Costco vs Walmart

	Costco	Walmart
People word mentions	96	136
Profit word mentions	281	517
People vs Profit ratios	1: 2.9	1: 3.8

Costco, a membership-based warehouse club, has a ratio of 1: 2.9 with 96 'people' mentions and 281 'profit' mentions, which implies a significant lean towards profit. This isn't surprising given the bottom-line-focused nature of retail. Yet, Costco's reputation within the retail industry as a 'people-first' employer somewhat juxtaposes this statistic. Known for providing higher-than-average wages and substantial benefits for its employees, Costco's annual report seems to downplay its people-centric ethos.

Over the years, Costco has maintained a largely scandal-free reputation, unlike many of its industry peers. This might indicate that its actions reflect a 'people-first' philosophy more accurately than its end of year report suggests. The company's emphasis on maintaining a loyal and motivated workforce aligns with its operational model that relies on membership loyalty and high-volume sales, reinforcing the importance of a people-centric approach even in a profit-focused industry.

Contrastingly, Walmart presents a ratio of **1: 3.8** with 136 'people' mentions and 517 'profit' mentions, demonstrating an even heavier profit-oriented slant. This outcome aligns with Walmart's reputation as a highly efficient, cost-driven entity. However, the company has often aced criticism for its alleged poor treatment of employees, which contradicts the ethos of a people-focused company.

Walmart's past is dotted with numerous lawsuits and scandals related to worker's rights, low wages, and poor working conditions. Despite recent efforts to improve its public image and implement more worker-friendly policies, the low 'people to profit' ratio could reflect existing narratives about Walmart prioritising profit over its workforce.

People and Profit Focused Trend

In Walmart's 2022 annual report, we can see that the profit-focus is still very much there. 2022 shows a ratio of **1: 3.2**, in comparison to 2021's **1: 3.8**, so whilst it does show an improvement, it seems Walmart still have a way to go.

- ✔ 2020 – **1: 4.3**
- ✔ 2021 – **1: 3.8**
- ✔ 2022 – **1: 3.2**

It also seems like they've come a fair way when you look at their 2020 report, which shows a ratio of **1: 4.3**. However, remember the average people to profit ratio is **1: 1**, which highlights how much work Walmart have to do.

Comparison #5: Kings of Cards: Mastercard vs VISA

	Mastercard	Visa
People word mentions	323	94
Profit word mentions	387	339
People vs Profit ratios	1: 1.2	1: 3.6

Visa, a giant in the payment technology space, reveals a **1: 3.6** ratio with 94 'people' mentions against 339 'profit' mentions, indicating a strong profit-oriented culture. Despite its consumer focused business model, Visa's communication seems heavily geared towards the company's profit-generating capabilities.

Over the years, Visa's reputation has been marred by several scandals related to monopolistic practices, price-fixing, and data breaches. These instances emphasise a 'profit over people' narrative that appears to overshadow Visa's efforts in corporate social responsibility, employee engagement, and customer-centric innovations. Visa's various scandals align with its lower 'people' mention ratio, suggesting that they might benefit from reorienting their annual report to reflect a more balanced approach and, in turn, their company culture.

On the contrary, Mastercard demonstrates a more people-focused trend with a ratio of **1: 1.2**, generated from 323 'people' mentions and 307 'profit' mentions. This considerably higher 'people' mention rate is surprising, given VISA's ratio, as it indicates a greater emphasis on human-centred aspects than what is typically expected in a financial corporation.

Mastercard's reputation is comparatively 'cleaner' than Visa's, although it has faced similar accusations of monopolistic behaviour and data breaches. However, the company has made significant efforts in recent years to rebrand itself as a technology company rather than a credit card conglomerate.

This transition may focus more on human-centric factors like talent acquisition, fostering innovation, and customer service. Hence, a higher ratio of 'people' mentions underscores this shift and reflects Mastercard's aim to position itself as a company that values people - employees, customers, or stakeholders - while maintaining a robust profit-making business model.

Excuse the interruption....

All this talk of profit may have you thinking about money, and nothing's free in this life, right?

Wrong!

The MBM website has a whole host of free resources for you and your team to utilise to become the best version of yourself.

Here's just a taste of what we can offer to you... for FREE!

- Over 1,000 Articles from Our Award Winning Blog.
- Personal Development Webinars.
- Whitepapers created specifically for HR Managers, L&D Managers & Training Officers.
- Over 700 One-Minute Personal Development videos on the MBM YouTube Channel.
- Sticky Learning Lunches that share tips on how to be the best version of yourself.
- Over 50 Helpful Infographics.

Comparison #6: Streaming Stepsisters: Netflix vs Disney

	Netflix	The Walt Disney Company
People word mentions	80	150
Profit word mentions	203	662
People vs Profit ratios	1 : 2.5	1 : 4.4

Netflix, with a people-to-profit ratio of 1 : 2.5 derived from 80 'people' mentions and 203 'profit' mentions, shows a profit focus, with more than twice as many profit mentions as people. This skew perhaps explains the criticism Netflix has faced for its keeper test culture where managers are encouraged to regularly evaluate their team members and part ways with those considered indispensable. This hire and fire culture, which seems to underscore a relentless pursuit of excellence at the expense of employee stability, may serve to reinforce Netflix's lean towards 'profit' in its communication.

#peoplevsprofit

Image from Disney Holidays.

However, in comparison to its Disney competitor, Netflix has less of a skew. Disney's commitment to creating an inclusive and diverse workspace, in recent years, and highlighting its initiatives in the areas of diversity and employee wellbeing, can account for this less drastic gulf between people and profit.

The Walt Disney Company presents an even more shocking profit focus with a ratio of 1: 4.4 based on 150 'people' mentions and a whopping 662 'profit' mentions. Disney, often referred to as 'The Happiest Place on Earth', has built its brand on creating magical experiences for people of all ages. However, the numbers suggest that the emphasis in their annual report appears to lean heavily towards profitability.

Did You Know?

Disney's slogan, 'The Happiest Place on Earth', was first coined in 1955 by Walt himself.

However, their annual report suggests that they may have abandoned this sense of magic to focus on the profit. What would Mickey say about that?!

The shift from Disney towards profit-centric communication could be attributed to their various high-stakes ventures, such as the expansion of its theme parks, the acquisition of 21st Century Fox, and the launch of its streaming service, Disney+ – a direct competitor for Netflix.

It's also important to note that Disney has not been immune to controversy, with scandals related to employee treatment, inadequate pay, and failure to address racial and cultural insensitivity in some of its content. The lower 'people' mention ratio in its communication might indicate an area where Disney could work to better align its annual report with its internal practices.

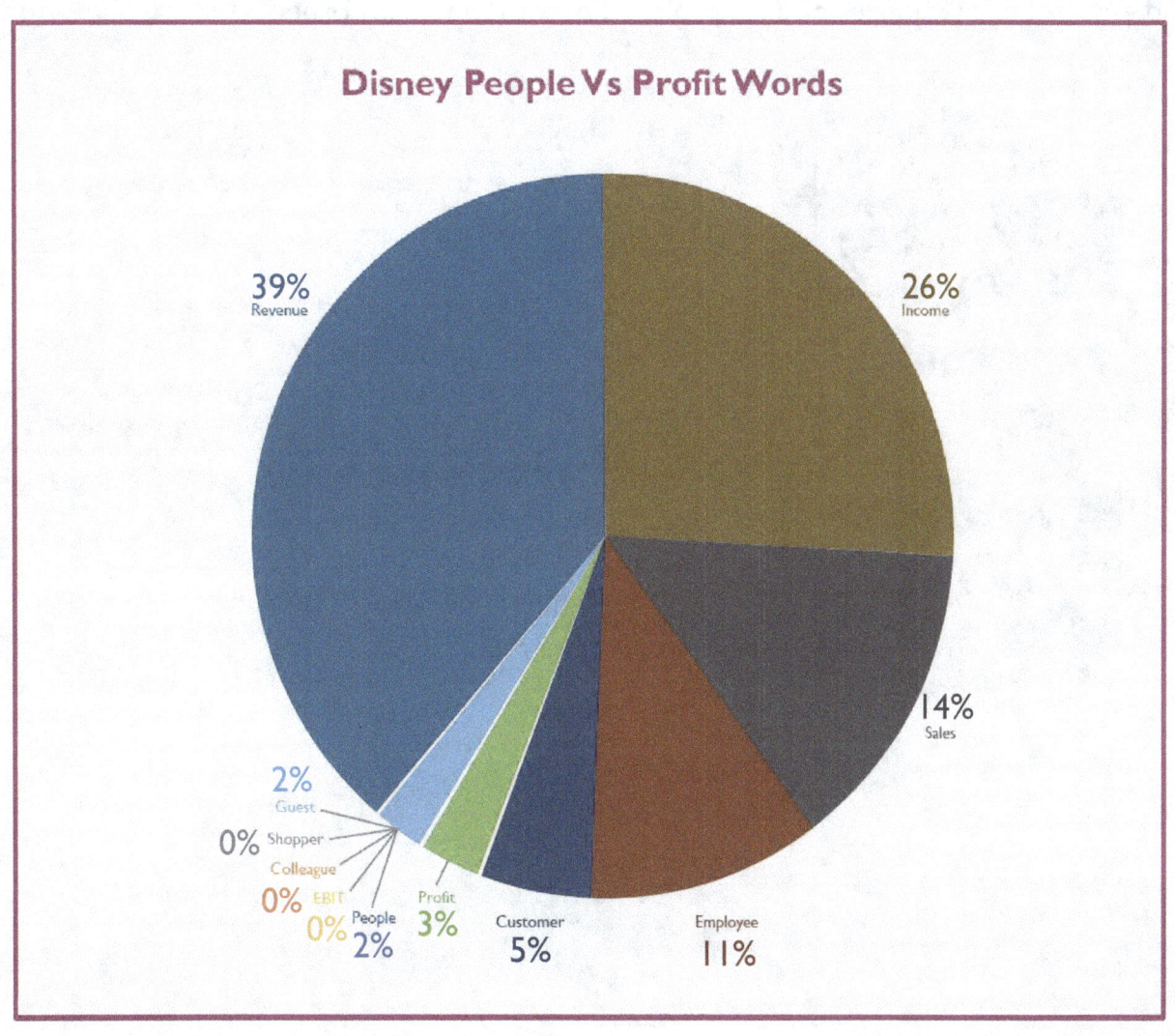

Disney People Vs Profit Words

39% Revenue

26% Income

14% Sales

11% Employee

5% Customer

3% Profit

2% People

0% EBIT

0% Colleague

0% Shopper

2% Guest

Indeed, the landscape is ever shifting. For instance, Netflix recently stirred up controversy when it announced plans to curtail password sharing among its users, a move many perceived as prioritising profit over user convenience. This change has already sparked considerable backlash and reignited discussions on the delicate balance between profitability and user satisfaction.

As a result, it's plausible that Netflix may need to shift the focus of its annual report to emphasise its commitment to its viewers more strongly. This potential shift towards a more people-centric skew would serve to reassure its user base that the company remains devoted to providing a service that meets their needs and values their loyalty. As such, it is a poignant reminder that companies must stay attuned to consumer sentiment and ensure their strategies balance profitability with the needs of people.

What may help Disney achieve a more people-centric ratio is better people management.

At MBM, we have a People Management course that will help you become a better people manager, thus allowing you to extract the maximum performance from your team.

Search 'People Management Course' on our website for more details.

Trust us, it's a course even Mickey would say 'Oh Boy!' to.

Comparison #7: Fight of the FMCGs: Unilever vs Procter & Gamble vs Nestle

	Unilever	Procter & Gamble	Nestle
People word mentions	454	181	63
Profit word mentions	644	402	247
People vs Profit ratios	1 : 1.4	1 : 2.2	1 : 3.9

With 454 'people' mentions and 644 'profit' mentions, Unilever presents a 'people to profit' ratio of 1 : 1.4, indicating a more balanced focus in their annual report. This emphasis on 'people' is perhaps not surprising given Unilever's ethos of humanity, a reputation that was further enforced by their 46 mentions of wellbeing in their annual report.

For instance, Unilever's Sustainable Living Plan placed people and planet alongside profit, which aligns well with their commitment to bettering lives, reducing environmental impact and improving health and wellbeing. The company's relative balance in 'people' and 'profit communications may reflect this integrated, people-centric strategy. That being said, the company hasn't been void of criticism, with the company being called out for greenwashing on multiple occasions.

Procter & Gamble and Nestle present a different narrative landscape. With a 'people' to 'profit' ratio of **1: 2.2** and **1: 3.9** respectively, these companies project a more profit-focused narrative. Nestle's 'people' focus may raise eyebrows given the company's various controversies over the years, including the infamous baby milk scandal in the 1970s. As per this data, the company's annual report could be interpreted as a tendency to prioritise profit over people, potentially reinforcing negative perceptions about its social responsibilities.

Procter & Gamble's annual report, much like Nestle's, leans towards profit. While Procter & Gamble is known for its brand innovation and market leadership, this lower people orientation may undermine its efforts in social responsibility. Interestingly, Procter & Gamble has been involved in some controversies related to environmental sustainability and labour violations. The predominance of 'profit' in their annual report could potentially exacerbate skepticism about their social and environmental commitments.

An interesting point to note is that, Nestle didn't make it to the top 50 of Fortune's 'Most Admired Companies' list, which is surprising given their balanced ratio. However, Nestle placed 41st and Procter and Gamble did even better, placing 24th. So, how can different ratings reflect their accomplishments so differently?

Image courtesy of The Global History of Capitalism

Talking of groceries, have you read our Rapid Groceries report? Head over to the 'Rapid Groceries' article on the MBM blog to download your FREE copy!

Do the Big Companies Care About Learning and Development?

Remember the sneaky extra sub-category that we mentioned earlier? Well, it's time to discuss it! As a reminder, we picked 5 learning and development words and searched the annual reports to see if, and how many times, they arose.

- Leadership
- Training
- Coaching
- Education
- Learning

The importance of continuous learning and development in today's rapidly evolving corporate landscape is undisputed. Notably, our study reveals that 'learning' garners significant attention in the annual reports of some companies, further spotlighting the shifting paradigms in today's corporate world. So, who came out on top in the world of learning and development?

Prosus NV, a global consumer internet group, tops the list with an impressive 103 mentions of 'learning.' This massive emphasis on learning could reflect the company's ambitious global growth strategy and its aim to stay at the forefront of the digital revolution. By championing continuous learning, Prosus NV might seek to foster a culture of innovation and agility, crucial for its survival and success in the fast-paced digital landscape.

Reliance Industries follows closely behind with 68 mentions of 'learning.' Reliance's emphasis on learning goes hand in hand with its focus on wellbeing, as evidenced in our previous section. This holistic approach, promoting learning and wellbeing, can be seen as a powerful tool for fostering a motivated, engaged, and resilient workforce, pivotal to the company's sustained success in a challenging and volatile business environment.

Next, we see Tata Consultancy Services, a well-known IT services and consulting company, who have a people to profit ratio of **1: 1.2**, and are spotlighting 'learning' 49 times. As with Reliance, Tata's focus on learning accompanies its slant toward wellbeing. By strongly emphasising wellbeing and learning, Tata seems to be crafting an employee-centric corporate culture, where personal growth and wellbeing are seen as two sides of the same coin. This dual focus highlights the company's commitment to nurturing its human capital and underscores the interconnectedness of wellbeing and learning as key drivers of employee engagement and productivity.

Take a look at the top 10 and bottom 10 companies for total learning words:

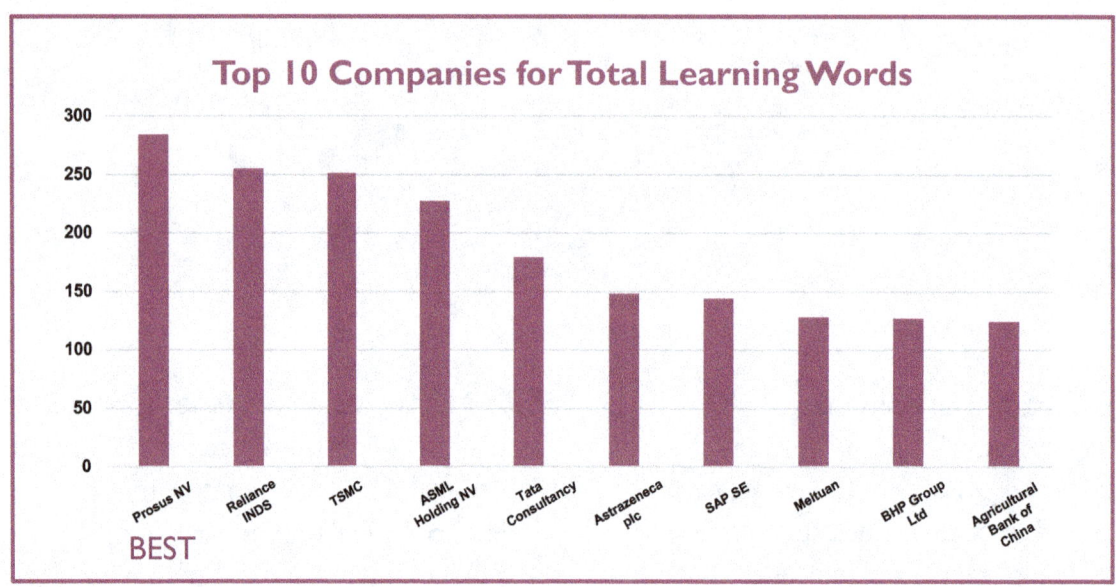

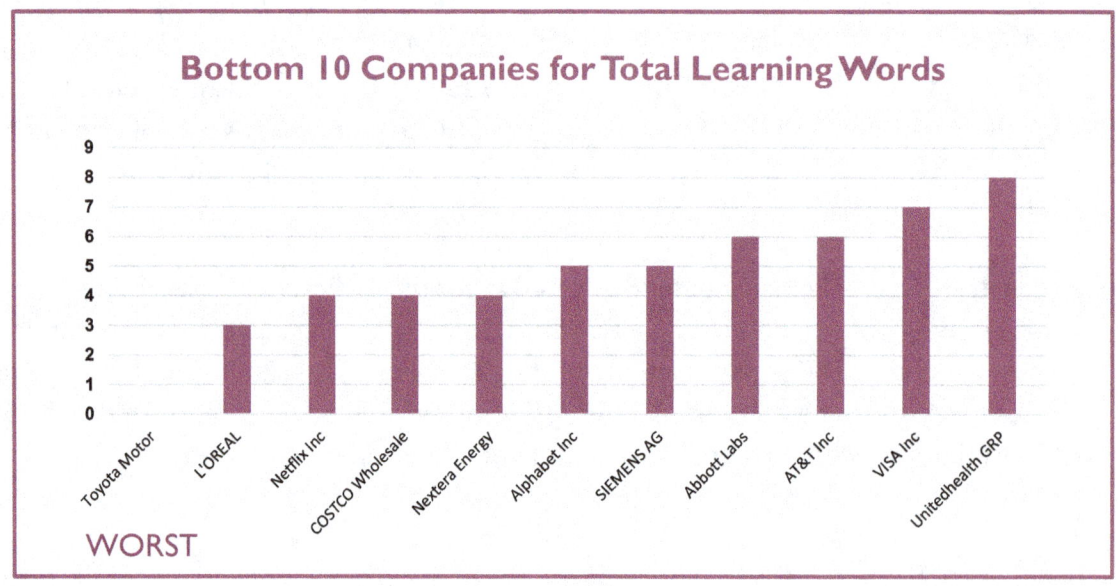

Prosus, Reliance and Tata's significant focus on 'learning', especially in conjunction with their emphasis on 'wellbeing,' underscores a growing trend in the corporate world. Companies are increasingly recognising the symbiotic relationship between continuous learning, wellbeing, and overall business success. It also speaks volumes about their commitment to employee development and understanding its ripple effects on organisational health and resilience.

Company	Learning Total	Learning Ranking	People Ranking	People to Profit Ratio
Prosus NV	284	#1	#6	1: 1.1
Reliance INDS	255	#2	#9	1: 1.3
TSMC	251	#3	#5	1: 1.3
ASML Holding	227	#4	#2	1: 0.6
Tata Consultancy	179	#5	#8	1: 1.2
AstraZeneca plc	148	#6	#30	1: 2.7
SAP SE	144	#7	#1	1: 0.9
Meituan	128	#8	#31	1: 1.7
BHP Group Ltd	127	#9	#16	1: 1.6
Agricultural Bank of China	124	#10	#11	1: 1.1

#peoplevsprofit

Insight #1: A Holistic Approach

One particularly interesting insight we found is that, of the above top 10 companies for learning and development mentions, 6 of these also feature in the top 10 ranking for people word mentions. This indicates that companies that are focusing on people have a very holistic approach and are tackling issues of learning and development also.

Insight #2: Not So Caring Healthcare?

Additionally, of the top 10 companies in learning and development, only 1 out of 10 are in the healthcare industry - AstraZeneca plc. This links to our findings in our topic analysis, and further rejects the assumption that healthcare companies have a people-centric attitude in their reports.

Insight #3: Training for the Right Reasons?

Most of the companies on the top 10 list are technology, banking, or science companies. Does this then suggest that those investing in learning and development are doing so for the profit benefits rather than the benefits to their employees?

Insight #4: Who Shows Learning Promise?

The stand out two companies from our table are AstraZeneca and BHP because they rank positions #30 and #31 for people to profit ratio, yet hold impressive learning rankings of #6 and #8 with learning mentions of 148 and 128 respectively.

Our earlier table looked at the top companies for 'learning' mentions alongside their ranking for 'people' mentions. In contrast, we wanted to do a similar piece of analysis but instead of 'learning and 'people' we wanted to flip the coin and look at 'learning' and 'profit'. By doing this, we are looking at both sides of the coin to see whether learning is synonymous with more profit-focused companies or people-focused companies.

Our table below looks at the top companies for 'learning' mentions and their ranking for the number of 'profit' mentions. Similarly to our previous table which compared 'learning' mentions to 'people' mentions, we now compare 'learning' mentions to 'profit' mentions. For example, SAP SE is #91, which means that they have one of the highest 'profit' mentions. Our eye-opener is that we would all assume companies with high 'learning' mentions would have a high number of 'people' mentions and a low mention of 'profit' words. Yet, what we see in our table below is that of the top 10 companies for 'learning' words, 7 of them are ranked #80 or above for highest 'profit' mentions'.

Company	Learning Total	Learning Ranking	Profit Ranking	People to Profit Ratio
Prosus NV	284	#1	#84	1:1.1
Reliance INDS	255	#2	#87	1:1.3
TSMC	251	#3	#90	1:1.3
ASML Holding	227	#4	#59	1:0.6
Tata Consultancy	179	#5	#83	1:1.2
AstraZeneca plc	148	#6	#96	1:2.7
SAP SE	144	#7	#91	1:0.9
Meituan	128	#8	#72	1:1.7
BHP Group Ltd	127	#9	#88	1:1.6
Agricultural Bank of China	124	#10	#71	1:1.1

The startling insight above, of the profit-focused companies using many 'learning' words, raises the question of motivation for training employees. For example, do companies train their employees for people development or because they know it creates a bigger return on investment?

And maybe, it doesn't matter.

If companies are training their people, and it makes the employee feel valued, and the bottom line is better, then that's a win for everyone.

A Spotlight on Leadership

Leadership and leadership skills are something we value highly at MBM, so we wanted to add in a special spotlight on how the top 100 are doing in terms of leadership within their annual reports.

Of the top 100 companies, AstraZeneca tops the list with 77 mentions of leadership. This is a surprising result as they have a people versus profit ratio of **1 : 2.7**, and not a great deal of people mentions. In fact, they mention 'leadership' almost as many times as they mention 'people'.

'People' companies on the list do not mention leadership at all: A1&1, China Construction Bank, Costco, L'Oreal and Toyota. We're going to shine a light on Toyota because their omission of 'leadership' from their annual report is particularly concerning considering their slogan 'Let's Go Places', recently replacing 'Moving Forward'. Both these slogans have a directional lexis, and the notion that they are the leader in taking us to those places. This is in direct contrast to the absence of 'leadership' in their annual report.

Similarly, one of Toyota's core production principles is 'Kaizen', which translates to 'continuous improvement'. The lack of 'leadership' mentions and of learning terms in general, with a total of zero, is shocking when considered in the context of 'Kaizen', which Toyota themselves claim 'humanises the workplace'. Continuous improvement suggests a strive towards bettering employees, learning more, a future focus. However, their annual report seems to reflect the opposite of 'Kaizen'.

Unlike, many of these other companies, Toyota seem to be missing out on offering a leadership programme or leadership training. For example, Reliance Industries, ranking second for leadership mentions, boasts a two-year leadership program that looks to nurture future leaders of Reliance.

"Despite talking the talk, many companies need to improve in walking the walk, especially in leadership. True success is not just about saying but doing—bridging the gap between words and actions. In the dance of profit and people, authentic leadership transforms intentions into a thriving reality." - **Kim-Adele Randall, CEO Authentic Achievements**

A Spotlight on Coaching

Similarly to leadership, coaching is kind of our thing and if you're looking to know why it should be your thing too, click on the video below.

Google conducted an extensive project called 'Project Oxygen'. In which Google reviewed and analysed over 10,000 performance documents. Their conclusion:

- Coaching is the skill that managers are poor at doing.
- Coaching is the skill managers need to be the best at doing.

As we're so passionate about coaching, we were very shocked that 65 out of 100 companies did not mention coaching at all in their annual reports. Considering we are in a climate of bettering ourselves and striving for improvement, both at work and personally, this is a shocking statistic, and one that 65 companies need to address.

Of these 65 companies that don't mention coaching, 4 of them are in the top 5 for market capitalisation, and they are worth over USD$1 trillion. They are; Apple, Aramco, Amazon and Alphabet.

AstraZeneca and Reliance Industries were ranked the highest and second highest for 'coaching' mentions, with 7 and 5 in total, respectively. These high mentions of coaching goes hand in hand with their high leadership mentions. AstraZenca stand at 77 'leadership' mentions, and Reliance at 74.

Interestingly, Pfizer, Coca-Cola and LVMH, which rank #2, #3 and #5 for overall people vs profit ratios, are amongst the 65 companies that fail to mention 'coaching'. This perhaps indicates that they are focusing on the wrong elements of people within their reports. It could suggest that they are mentioning 'people' in relation to the profits that they can create as opposed to the development and wellbeing of them.

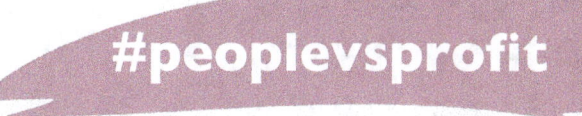

#peoplevsprofit

Excuse the interruption....

Do you think that your company could be alongside those 65 that simply forgot about coaching in their annual report?

If that's the case, we have just the thing to get you started on that crucial coaching journey.

This deck of coaching cards is one of over 25, each with their own specific topic to help you to become the best version of yourself.

Our coaching cards are easy to use, simply follow these 10 steps:

1. Booking a meeting with your interviewee/ coachee (that could be yourself) for 30-60 minutes.
2. At the start of your session explain to your coachee that this is a coaching session:
   -They should bear with you as you learn and get used to coaching with the cards.
   -You will invite them to give you feedback at the end.
   -Ask them to keep an open mind.
   -here might be some bumps and pauses as this is a new approach to personal development or coaching.
3. Start with the whole deck of +100 cards in front of you. Set your instructions cards to one side. Shuffle through and separate your
4. cards into 4 piles.

5. Begin with the Equity coaching cards in your hand.
6. Pick out the most appropriate questions from these first 20 cards. You do not need to ask all 20 questions, and you do not need to ask them in the order you have found them. Your aim is to help the coachee to identify their goal.
7. Start asking and see what comes up.
8. Repeat the above steps for the other 3 stages; Diversity, Inclusion and Belonging.
9. Finish the coaching session when you have a clear answer in each stage.
10. The final step is to get some feedback for yourself and the coach.

A Company Comparison Spotlight: ASML vs Pfizer

The training and development mentions offered by companies can provide great insights into their true dedication to a people-first approach.

Pfizer, for example, provides insights into its training and development approach on its website, where it discusses personal development plans, its active mentoring promotion practices, emphasises internal advancement, provides short & medium-term experiential opportunities, and offers learning and development opportunities. Nevertheless, the company is rather vague, and does not provide in-depth information on how exactly employees carry out these options.

ASML, on the other hand, approaches development and training from a more cultural aspect. In other words, it incorporates learning and development as part of its core values. Its website mentions 'supporting you to make a difference', and playing an active role in the communities they operate in, while paying close attention to wellbeing. In fact, its website highlights the following:

'At ASML, we value high-performance individuals with a strong focus on wellbeing. Your health and work-life balance come first, and we support you in achieving your true potential and staying happy and thriving'.

There is a clear difference here: wellbeing and professional development go hand in hand with working for ASML, whereas it seems Pfizer's approach to development and training is one that incorporates it as an addition to the job.

Excuse the interruption....

Has all this talk about learning and development got you wondering how you could improve your team's training? Then look no further than Sticky Learning ®.

The leaky bucket image represents the way we all currently learn. A lot goes in and then goes straight out. This is why we developed 'Sticky Learning ®'. After 30 days, you could lose up to 80% of what you have learnt, unless you you use space repetition to make your learning stick.

With us, learners will make changes in their behaviours because of Sticky Learning ®. We built it using 14 learning sciences and we are still non-stop pushing the boundaries of stickiness.

Visit our website today to find out more about how Sticky Learning ® can start you on the journey to becoming the best version of yourself.

Training Provider A

Learning

Training Provider B

Sticky Learning

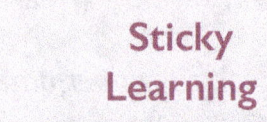

What Do the Words Count For?

You might naturally assume that all company annual reports are a similar length, effectively providing the same quantity of information. However, this is far from reality. For example, why does VISA's annual report have only 63,103 words, while Unilever has over double that with 138,85? Or even more drastic, why is T-Mobile's report (260,619 words) 43 times longer than L'Oréal's (6,049 words)?

The answer could simply be because there is no set limit or minimum criteria for an annual report – which is possibly part of the problem.

We've selected the five lowest and the five highest word counts across the 100 companies and compiled them into the below graph to highlight the disparity.

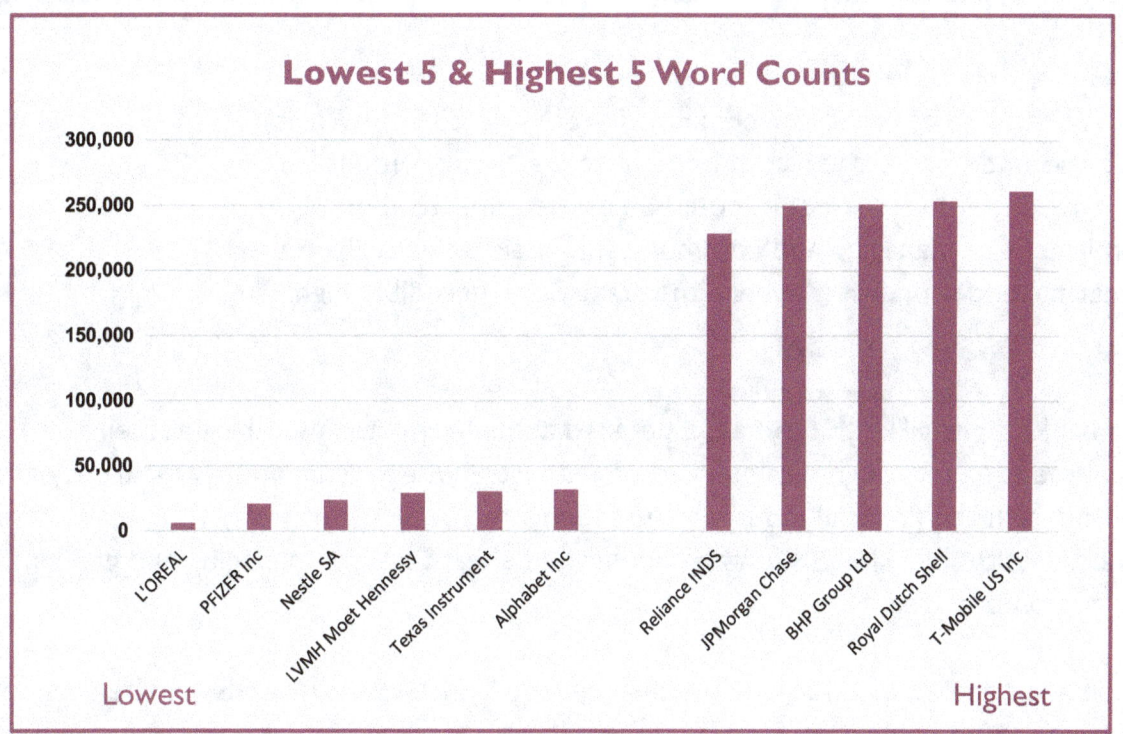

However, there are many other reasons that may also contribute to the variation in word count. When you see a company such as BHP Group (250,786 words), a leading global resources company, presenting a comprehensive annual report, it could suggest a conscious effort to maintain a high level of transparency. Their expansive report might reflect their diverse business activities across various sectors and regions, and a testament to their commitment to keeping stakeholders informed about all aspects of the business.

Did You Know?

In the last five years, company's annual reports have ballooned in size by 46%.

The average report is adding 5,800 words and 8 pages every year.

Similarly, the size of Bristol-Myers annual accounts (83,216 words) might also underscore their commitment to risk management. The company's extensive disclosure could be a testament to their commitment to managing and communicating risks effectively in the biopharmaceutical industry, where the stakes are incredibly high.

For a banking giant like JP Morgan, a detailed annual report can underline their commitment to thorough disclosures in an industry where trust and transparency are paramount. In the financial industry, trust forms the bedrock of every transaction. Financial institutions like JP Morgan handle the delicate task of managing and growing their customers' wealth.

The detailed nature of JP Morgan's annual report, with 249,890 words, can be seen as an attempt to instill confidence in their stakeholders. By providing extensive information on their operations, financial performance, and strategic direction, maybe they are essentially saying 'We have nothing to hide'.

Interestingly, 4 of the annual reports in our pool of companies have a lower word count than this report; L'Oréal, Nestle, Pfizer and LVMH.

Final Thoughts to Takeaway

In 2023, the state of the global economy is on a shaky road. For companies to remain relevant, and for employees to continue wanting to be employed there, efforts must be sustained to create engaging workplaces. Unfortunately, as seen throughout this report, this is not always the case. So, where do we go from here? How can companies improve their standing and become more people-focused? This is where increased investments in employee engagement comes in.

What are the big takeaways? Perhaps it is that companies, following Covid-19, must make employee satisfaction – and hence investments in their people – more of a priority. Or, perhaps it is that we need to take notes from companies we didn't expect would do so well, like the more junior tech company, SAP SE, or the American giant, JP Morgan.

One commonality that we found was that there are clear disparities between popular opinion and actual company reports. Fortune and their top lists say one thing, but our data shows us something else, which is troubling. And that is, that not enough companies focus on 'people', or at least that is our conclusion having interrogated their annual reports.

Understanding what makes some companies more prone to focusing on their people versus profit can teach us how to ensure our people are happier than ever. Of course, some aren't so surprising – Samsung, for example, could take some lessons on becoming more people focused, but that may be too optimistic…maybe.

My initial curiosity drove us to analyse the top 100 global companies' annual reports to identify whether they were profit or people focused. Before we started this mammoth journey, we had to accept two assumptions.

Firstly, that annual reports were the last untouched communication from a company's heart and soul to the public. Unaffected by the bods in marketing. Almost an intravenous drip into the company's psyche.

The second assumption was that the annual reports were, let's call it, the leadership voice. A communication channel where the Chairman and Directors could allow their inner-most thoughts and feelings to be voiced without barriers.

Having spent the last 18 months with my team on this project, we have been astounded by the spectrum of people to profit ratio (1: 0.3 to 1: 7.1) which has led us to continually debate whether a) the annual report mirrors the company culture or b) whether the annual report is disconnected from the company culture. Our analysis concluded, using the people to profit ratio, whether the company was people to profit focused. Then, we dove deeper into some companies to see whether the annual report truly did mirror the company culture or not.

My hopes are that we have not opened Pandora's Box, which would mean that the marketing gurus grab hold of the annual accounts and tell us more of what they want to tell us. I still want companies to be transparent and authentic in their annual report. So, instead, I hope that annual reports can, either 1) more mirror their company culture, focus and ethos, or 2) improve their company culture which then, in turn, is mirrored in the annual report.

Plus, of course, my hope is that these companies reach out to us so that we can help them (all employees) to be the very best version of their soft skills self.

7 Main Takeaways

1. 85 out of 100 companies focus more on profit than people in their annual reports, even in today's climate of emphasising employee happiness. This can be evidenced by their ratio of more than **1 : 1**.

2. Wellbeing and mental are issues that many companies are simply glossing over in their annual accounts. 21 companies do not mention wellbeing, wellness, or mental health at all in their 2021 annual reports.

3. Across all the topics that we looked at in this report, a common theme was disparity between the values in which companies claim to focus on in other outward communication, and the focus of their annual report. A key example of this is Toyota, who claims 'Kaizen' as one of their core values, meaning 'continuous improvement', and yet have a total of zero learning mentions.

4. There is a very large spectrum for green mentions within the top 100 companies with the highest number of green mentions coming in at 760 (SAP SE) and the lowest number of mentions being 4 (Netflix).

5. With today's working world having an increasing focus on learning and development, one of the more surprising insights was that 5 companies do not mention 'leadership at all in their annual report.

6. Google's Project Oxygen concluded that the one skill line managers are poor at is coaching, but the one skill they should be best at is coaching. With this in mind, it's quite shocking to learn that 65% of the top global companies, leave out coaching completely from their 2021 annual reports.

7. With L'Oréal's report being 43 times shorter than T-Mobile's, it seems as though annual reports have no rhyme or reason for their length.

The final thing to say would be a special mention to Roche Holdings and Dr. Christoph Franz for achieving the #1 spot in our people to profit ratio league table - a big well done!

Welcome to the World's Stickiest Learning

Here at MBM, we have some major solutions available for you, the biggest being Sticky Learning ®. We pride ourselves on being the World's Stickiest Learning because we incorporate strategies like the 70:20:10 model to achieve behavioural change that sticks.

Stickiest Learning

We specialise in 'people' focused investment for short and long-term results and goals. Companies who recognise the need to focus on their people in terms of coaching and development can partner with us. We have worked alongside many big names, such as the NHS, Vodafone, and Pokémon. We are the solution for you.

By using the training and coaching cards available through MBM, you can begin to show your company your commitment to investing in your human resources. Your team members and the company can greatly benefit from our amazing resources that generate results and create longevity. Have a look at www.makingbusinessmatter.co.uk for all the options we have available.

Excuse the interruption....

If you liked this report, and want to hear more from us then how about pre-ordering our newest book, Swat That Fly? Or taking a look at our previous work on 78 Persuasion Techniques?

'Swat That Fly' has a testimonial from Brian Tracy, best-selling author of 'Eat That Frog'!

"Fully 30% of your time is spent in meetings - one-on-one, or in groups, and most of the time is wasted with unclear goals and poor follow-up. This remarkable book shows you practical, proven methods and techniques to multiply your results and become an invaluable resource in getting more done, faster, for yourself and your company."

Brian Tracy – Consultant, Author, Speaker
Book launching January 2024!

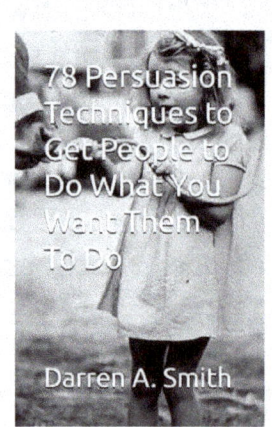

available at

Interested in the Specifics?

If you're interested in the breakdown of the people vs profit word mentions, like the mention of a specific word, then we've got you covered. Plus, take a look at any topic that you're particularly interested in; wellbeing, mental health or, sustainability perhaps.

Here's a sneak peek at our database of the 100 companies with all the information you need (or perhaps ever wanted!).

Click on the image below to be taken to our full database:

Company	Industry	Well-being	People	Employee	Colleague	Shopper	Guest	Customer	People Total
Abbott Labs	Medical device	0	35	10	0	0	0	37	82
Abbvie Inc	Pharma	2	25	207	1	0	0	42	275
Accenture plc	IT	5	84	91	0	0	0	18	193
Adobe Inc	Technology	6	14	111	0	0	0	395	520
Agricultural Bank of China	Bank	0	39	142	2	0	0	427	610
AIA	Insurance	6	58	160	1	0	0	166	385
Alibaba GRP	Technology	0	64	180	0	0	1	214	459
Alphabet Inc	Technology	0	29	7	0	1	0	25	62
Amazon	Technology	0	24	43	1	0	0	197	265
Amgen Inc	Medical device	5	24	55	1	0	0	40	120
Anheuser-Busch	Brewing	1	39	128	31	0	0	72	270
Apple	Technology	0	1	67	0	0	0	53	121
ASML Holding NV	Science	15	147	362	12	0	1	529	1051
Astrazeneca plc	Pharma	3	92	272	5	0	1	43	413
AT&T Inc	Telecommunication	0	8	63	1	0	0	148	220
Bank of America	Bank	3	36	153	6	0	0	104	299
Bank of China	Bank	3	62	100	1	1	0	414	578
Berkshire Hathaway	Insurance	0	14	18	0	0	0	182	214
BHP Group Ltd	Mining	18	171	305	2	0	0	66	544
Boeing Co	Aircraft	0	9	95	3	0	0	370	477
Bristol-Myer SQB	PHARma	6	9	285	1	0	0	77	372
Broadcom Inc	Technology	0	1	90	0	0	0	330	421
Charter Communications	Telecommunication	0	3	57	0	0	0	437	497
Chevron Corp	Car	0	9	44	0	0	0	26	79
China Construction Bank	Bank	0	6	18	1	0	0	156	181

Sponsor: The Frank Bruno Foundation

The Frank Bruno Foundation was founded as a direct result of the former heavy weight Champion of the world, Frank Bruno, wanting to create a positive change in communities.

Frank has spoken openly of the vital role exercise has played in his battle with mental ill-health and is now driven to help others battle their own mental health challenges. Frank wanted to help support those struggling with early-stage mental ill health as well as raise awareness of causes that may contribute to mental ill health.

Image supplied by
The Frank Bruno Foundation.

The Frank Bruno Foundation exists to provide support, encouragement, and the motivation to succeed for those currently facing or recovering from early-stage mental ill health issues. The Foundation aims to achieve this by providing opportunities to participate in non-contact boxing and mental health and wellbeing workshops offering clients the tools to manage their own mental health individually with strategies tailored to them.

'Absolutely brilliant place that supports the local community'

~ Kimberley R ~

'Big appreciation to all the staff at The Frank Bruno Foundation. You have been first class and deserve recognition. Through your classes I am learning to let go of the past. Thank you'.

~ Leanne ~

🌐 info@thefrankbrunofoundation.co.uk

🌐 www.thefrankbrunofoundation.co.uk

Sponsor: Mentl Awards

At Mentl we believe that everyone should thrive. We believe in having honest, open conversations.

We believe in tackling the stigma of mental health, whether in the workplace or in our community.

Our vision is a world where no one feels that they need to be brave to talk about mental health or seek consultations, because mental health and mental healthcare are a part of our relationships, routine, and rhetoric. Our vision is a world where mental health is health.

We promise to be a trusted place for all people navigating mental health by leading the conversation to normalise mental health.

'Join our mission to make all health mental health. It's time to tackle the stigma head on. It's time for open, honest conversations. It's time for us all to thrive'.

Image from the Mentl Awards page.

We've created the Mentl Awards for our dose of inspiration. Join us in celebrating the passionate people behind amazing projects.

- ⊕ hello@mentl.space
- ⊕ https://mentl.space

Thank You to Our Contributors

We wanted to dedicate a page in this report to everyone that helped bring this research to life. So, a huge thank you to following people who spent countless hours researching, moulding, and shaping this report so that we could bring to you the best possible version.

Gabby Smith

Gabby is a recent graduate of Media and Communications from Loughborough University, with experience in PR, marketing, and publishing. She enjoys bringing the industry of soft skills to life through blogging and SEO for MBM.

 | https://www.linkedin.com/in/gabriella-scarlet-smith

George Araman

George Araman is a content & communication specialist with 13 years of experience in the fields of marketing and self-improvement. He holds a master's degree, 21+ certificates, and is a certified Canfield Trainer. George also wrote an international bestselling book.

 | https://www.linkedin.com/in/georgearaman

Ailish O'Rourke Henriette

With over 20 years' experience in Hospitality, L&D, Quality Assurance and Recruitment in international locations with diverse and dynamic teams. Excited to share my experience and know-how with eager readers.

 | https://www.linkedin.com/in/ailish-o-rourke-henriette-22bb151b

Annabelle Cole

With a degree in Graphic Communication and Illustration from Loughborough University, design agency experience, Annabelle is a freelance Graphic Designer who enjoys working on branding, social media graphics, animation, and producing high-quality, creative outcomes for clients.

 | https://www.linkedin.com/in/annabelle-cole-35a48a202

About the Author

Hi, my name is Darren A. Smith, Founder of Making Business Matter (MBM) – The soft skills training provider.

I have always been fascinated by what people say. Their use of power words, like my example of Dad (God rest him) saying 'Don't run' and that if we could create a word cloud of all that was said in a company, how different would they look? That's where we arrived at annual reports. They are less marketing-y than the corporate websites which tell you what they want to tell you, or the tv advertisements that really tell you what they want to tell you. Annual accounts have a less marketing feel about them. Yes, some are glossy and possibly scripted, yet it still feels like the last bastion of a company talking about itself without being dictated by what they just want us to hear.

Darren A. Smith

Founder & CEO
Making Business Matter
(MBM)

Having begun down this road 18 months ago and now arriving at the analysis we have, many companies seemed to have mirrored themselves perfectly, and others possibly not. Surely, no marketing department would allow a company not to mention wellbeing, wellness, or mental health in 191,242 words (ahem – Alibaba!). Or, allow a company to communicate a focus that is too heavy on profit when we know that prospective talent reads annual reports before choosing the company they want to work for.

We may have created a monster. By analysing the annual accounts in this way, maybe companies will now market them better, rather than them being an innocent reflection of who they are. I hope not, because transparency, honesty and authenticity are still the watchwords for any company and rather than make the tail wag the dog, I am sure we'd all rather that wellbeing, mental health, and a balanced profit & people approach were the company's culture and not just one that they wanted us to believe.

I hope you found this report as fascinating to read as we did to produce it. Thank you for reading. Come and connect with me.

 | https://www.linkedin.com/in/darrenantonysmith

Sponsor: Storeyline Resumes

storeyline resumes

| www.storeylineresumes.com | 724-832-8845 | www.linkedin.com/in/robynnstorey |

Storeyline Resumes has been in business for 23 years and we have developed over 350,000 resumes for clients primarily in the senior level and executive space. Our writing, interviewing and coaching team is USA-based and comprised of business executives from every industry. We are ranked #1 on LinkedIn for best, most cost effective and quality for both Senior and Executive Resumes/LinkedIn Profiles and we work with executive clients from around the world. Schedule a call with us today!

GET NOTICED WITH A KILLER RESUME!

Our team is here to tell your story the RIGHT way.

CALL OR TEXT TO GET STARTED TODAY!
(724-832-8845)

Thank you for reading.
Please share this report with others.

You can download a free digital copy via this link:

https://www.makingbusinessmatter.co.uk/people-vs-profit

#peoplevsprofit

World's Stickiest Learning

We are the soft skills training provider, partnering with clients that are frustrated by their people returning from training courses and then doing nothing differently. Our clients choose us because we achieve behavioural change through our unique training method, Sticky Learning ®.

Share this report

- ⊕ https://www.makingbusinessmatter.co.uk
- ⊕ https://www.linkedin.com/company/making-business-matter
- ⊕ https://www.youtube.com/makingbusinessmatter.co.uk